Adaptable

Praise for Adaptable

"Alexa is the authentic leader we all need. The vulnerable stories she shares in *Adaptable* won't just leave readers feeling inspired; but they will also walk away with the right tools to actually change their life for the better." - **Elena Cardone**, best-selling author and founder of 10X Ladies

"If you think that achieving your dreams is impossible, Alexa will change your mind—and she will change your life. In these pages, she will help you discover who you are, what you're meant to achieve in the world, and how to turn your vision into a reality." - **Dr. Kellyann Petrucci**, *New York Times* best-selling author of *Dr. Kellyann's Bone Broth Diet,* host of the PBS special, *21 Days to a Slimmer, Younger You,* and creator of drkellyann.com

"Alexa Carlin is the real deal. Authentic, approachable, inspiring as heck, and a true leader for women. The stories within *Adaptable* will move you to tears, inspire you to view life with a positive perspective, and empower you to keep going." - **Jessica Zweig**, best-selling author of *Be.* and CEO of SimplyBe. Agency

"*Adaptable* is hopeful, funny, and wise, and will remind you of who you are and what you can be. Through personal experience gained the hard way, Alexa delivers raw and vulnerable stories combined with catalyzing questions, helping you to build a framework that will allow you to become everything you've ever dreamed you could be, and everything you never dared dream was possible. If you feel like you are on the cusp of something bigger, this book is your next must-read."- **Laura Gassner Otting**, *Washington Post* best-selling author of *Limitless: How to Ignore Everybody, Carve Your Own Path, and Live Your Best Life*

"Adaptable is a must-read to help you turn any obstacle into an opportunity. Alexa writes with such vulnerability and authenticity it feels like you're listening to your best friend share their deepest stories with you. This book will inspire you to take action on your biggest dreams and help you persevere regardless of the challenges that come your way."- **Magie Cook**, international speaker, author, Nobel Prize Winner and CEO of Magie Cook, LLC

"Empowering, real, raw, and game-changing! Alexa's stories within *Adaptable* will remind you of the potential you hold inside of you and the strength to push through any obstacle. An inspiring book by an inspiring woman!" - **Jess Ekstrom**, author of *Chasing the Bright Side*

"Adaptable is a must read for anyone trying to silence that negative voice in their head and go after their dreams. Alexa's voice is so real, inspiring, and motivating that you can't help but feel empowered to live your best life." - **Rachel DeAlto**, author of *relatable*, Relationship Expert, and television personality

"Adaptable is a book in which every reader will feel as though the book is speaking directly to them; it will feel like a dialogue with a close friend. This is because Alexa Carlin is one of the most authentic and approachable human beings on the planet. A true leader is one that leads by empowering others... and that is exactly who Alexa is which in turn doesn't surprise me on how much more empowered reading the book has already made me feel!" - **Jordana Guimarães**, co-founder of Fashinnovation and founder of The NYLON Project

"Alexa's real-life truth telling will empower you to become the best version of yourself. Authentic, real, vulnerable, and powerful! *Adaptable* helps readers re-discover the hope, strength, and courage within their heart." - **Jen Gottlieb**, co-founder, Super Connector Media

"*Adaptable* is the empowering message you didn't know you needed, and Alexa is the voice perfectly suited to deliver it. This is the read that will finally convince you that there is nothing you can't handle in this life." - **Michelle Dempsey-Multack**, coach and author of *Moms Moving On: Real Life Advice on Conquering Divorce, Co-Parenting Through Conflict, and Becoming Your Best Self*

"This book is for those dreamers who know they're meant to do big things, yet are constantly hit with one challenge after the next. *Adaptable* is the book to help any dreamer push through the obstacles and find their way again." - **Amanda Perna**, founder and creative director of The House of Perna and Neon Bohemians, two-time *Project Runway* designer, and globally recognized TV personality

"POWER. CHAMPION. INSPIRATION. LOVE. RESILIENCE. HUMOR. These are a few immediate thoughts that come to mind in *Adaptable*. It's THE book to read to find the hope and light again, regardless of the where you are in life, or where you're headed! Throughout the book, you hear authenticity and desire which is always a winning combination of an inspiring life coach and your very best friend." – **Simon T. Bailey**, author of *Be the Spark*

Adaptable

*How to Lead with Curiosity, Pivot with
Purpose, and Thrive through Change*

WEX PRESS
womenempowerX

ALEXA CARLIN

WEX PRESS
womenempowerX.

A Collaboration Imprint with GracePoint Publishing
(www.GracePointPublishing.com)

GracePoint Matrix, LLC
624 S. Cascade Ave #201
Colorado Springs CO 80903
www.GracePointMatrix.com
Email: Admin@GracePointMatrix.com
SAN # 991-6032

Library of Congress Control Number: 2021902893

ISBN-13: (Paperback) – 978-1-951694-39-5
eISBN: (eBook) - 978-1-951694-40-1

Cover photo and About the Author photo by Debra Gloria Photography
All other images created by Author

Books may be purchased for educational, business, or sales promotional use.
For bulk order requests and price schedule contact:
Orders@GracePointPublishing.com

Dedication

To my mom, dad, and sister,
for never giving up on me,
or each other,
and showing me what true strength,
love, and resilience looks like.

Table Of Contents

For a long time, I was searching for the light at the end of the tunnel, until I finally realized the light was within me all along.

Introduction

❝We have to induce your daughter into a medical coma. Call your family, she has 24 hours to live.❞ This is what the doctors told my mom when I was just 21 years old. I was in college, growing one of my first businesses, and only months away from graduation when out of nowhere, deadly bacteria entered my system sending my body into septic shock and changing the course of my entire life.

It was this huge life-altering experience that led me to years of personal tragedy, loss, and ongoing obstacles—all at such a young age. And for a long time, I allowed this to define me. For a long time, I allowed this circumstance to stop me. But through the years if I've learned anything that I can share with you that has changed my life, it's that your obstacles can do one of two things: They can either push you back or fuel you forward. And the decision is up to you.

The power of your reality is always in your control simply by understanding the power of your thoughts, the power in how you perceive the world.

That's what I hope this book will teach you; how to shift your perception so regardless of the obstacles and challenges you experience, you have the knowledge, strength, and understanding of how to adapt so you can then thrive.

Too many people are teaching others from a place of success, meaning they share only what they overcame in the past. I'm here sharing vulnerably from inside the hardship. I did not fully overcome my past tragedies because from them, I now live with an ongoing chronic autoimmune disease, which is something I'm never going to be able to overcome. It's always easier when looking back, but what if you can live the life you've always imagined even while going through the challenges?

That's the power of learning how to adapt. There's power in leading your life with a curious soul, pivoting based on your purpose, and thriving through any change.

You don't have to wait to overcome anything to be who you are meant to be. You can do that right here and right now. Throughout this book, each lesson is first shared with you through a personal story. I don't want you to only see the highlight reel and the post-lesson me, I want you to see the real me; the one who struggles with self-doubt, fear, and insecurity.

I designed each chapter intentionally with a heartfelt share, a personal story, the lesson learned, one powerful quote I want to drive home, and an action step that will help you take that lesson and implement it into your life for immediate results.

This book is meant to be consumed in two ways. First, read it from front to back. Second, use it as a tool to help you find hope when it may be lost, to help you through times of self-doubt when pursuing your dreams, or for a beacon of light during some difficult times. Keep it near and anytime you feel you need a reminder, randomly flip open to a new chapter while asking for the answer you're looking for, and read whatever chapter opens up.

That's the power of learning how to adapt

Everyone goes through life with different experiences, the key is to continuously adapt through all the changes so you can always rise above the obstacles.

Obstacles, by definition, can block one's way or hinder progress. Many people experience challenges that differ from the stories shared within this book. May we all educate ourselves on the various ways people live and continue to use our voices to help evolve the world for the better. This book is meant as a journey

I believe in the power of you, the power of one

of self-awareness and a tool to analyze your own internal dialogues, and, when you feel something resonates with you, implement the changes recommended.

I believe in the power of you, the power of one. That one person, one decision, one book can possibly change your life for the better, forever. But you must be curious enough to discover that one. This book may be it. One quote in the book may be it. You sharing a highlight from an excerpt in this book on your social media may be that one thing to someone else.

Continue to spread your light; it's creating ripple effects of positive change in the world. Share what resonates with you in this book with others. Share it with me, I'd love to hear your thoughts!

My intention is that everything I've learned, all the hardships I've experienced, and the vulnerable moments I've shared with you in this book are of some service to you. I hope it helps you find the light within you. I hope you can see just how strong and resilient you are. I hope it helps you share your authentic self with the world. And above all I hope you never give up. Never give up on yourself or your dreams.

There is power behind your thoughts and we must empower one another to keep going, against all odds.

No more excuses. No more waiting. No more wishing, wondering or living in the past.

Regardless of how many times you get knocked down, keep standing up. Regardless of the odds against you, keep believing in yourself.

They gave me a one percent chance to live, and here I am. The odds have not always been in my favor, but they didn't need to be - because all you need is one.

You are the one percent, the one percent that can change the world.

Xx Alexa

P.S. Connect with me while reading this book. I would love to be on the journey with you. @AlexaRoseCarlin

P.P.S. This is just the beginning.

CHAPTER ONE

The Greatest Comeback

Your life isn't defined by how many times you succeed, but rather how many times you fall and decide to get back up.

Life, people, events may knock you down, but they can only keep you down if you decide to let them. Nothing can defeat you without your permission.

This self-evident truth should be something you hold on to in order to push forward and chase after what you want in this life, yet the fear and uncertainty of the knockdowns hold so many people back. You have the power to always rise again and to be straightforward with yourself, no amount of "playing it safe" will keep you from the hardships of life.

You can't escape it. You can't hide from it. So, you may as well do what you want while you are here. Take risks. Dream big and then dream bigger. Try something new. Speak up. Stand tall. Go on an adventure. Get lost. Get found. Be goofy. Color outside the lines. Just do *you*.

Because at the end of the day, no matter what you do or what you experience, you have a choice: Stay knocked down or get back up.

The decision is up to you. You *do* have the strength, you *do* have the power, you *do* have the potential to bounce back.

◆◆◆

There is no way around the fact that life will knock you down, but you don't have to let it keep you down. It is your job to train yourself and your mind to have the strength to always rise again.

I could have easily stayed down. I was knocked down one tragedy after the next for seven straight years.

My victim mindset, the triggers of post-traumatic stress, and the fear are consistent companions that I must negotiate with each day. They are very much a part of who I am, but they do not define what I can or cannot do.

I would love to say I had one huge knockdown and since then have been able to come back stronger than ever, yet this is farthest from the truth.

Because I haven't had just one knockdown, I've been knocked down over and over and over again.

And I'm still going through the knockdowns.

I don't have all the answers figured out or have this "perfect" life, but regardless, I'm still chasing after my dreams. I'm deciding every single day to stand back up because that is what you must do in order to live the life you deserve.

And I hope this book will help you make the same decision on your own journey.

For seven straight years I experienced one hit after another. From my sister almost taking her own life, to my near-death experience being given a one percent chance to live, to my dad losing his business, to a close relative relapsing on drugs, to my parents splitting up briefly, to my family dog's sudden death, then the external family disowning my own family, followed by getting diagnosed with an autoimmune disease, then struggling with this debilitating illness, to countless hospital stays, and multiple moves across the country, to lots and lots of loss, heartbreak, and obstacles ...

I lived in fear every day for those seven years. Every time my mom called just to say hello my heart began to race as the PTSD (post-traumatic stress disorder) would trigger and I'd be nervous to hear what she had to say on the phone, nervous that again, something bad was happening. (And my mom called me probably ten to twenty times a day.)

It took me a very long time and a lot of strength to try and come out of this constant fear and I'll be honest, I'm still working on it. I'm not completely free from living in the past because it's so engrained inside of me.

When I was twenty-one years old, I had a near-death experience that changed my entire life, when a deadly bacteria got into my bloodstream and left me in a coma fighting for my life in the intensive care unit with only a one-percent chance of survival. I thought that this was the one big knockdown I'd have to overcome, yet six months after that I was diagnosed with a debilitating chronic illness, ulcerative colitis. Now this was the hardest thing I'd ever have to try and come back from.

Each time I thought I was on the path to remission, I'd get knocked down again.

One year after my near-death experience and a few months after being diagnosed with ulcerative colitis, I moved back home to South Florida to gain the support of my family. I left all my dreams in New York City behind, thinking that would be a fresh start. Yet a few weeks after the move, my grandma passed away and I found myself again in the hospital diagnosed with yet another illness.

Each time I thought I was on the path to remission, I'd get knocked down again

This is just one of many moments where I was trying to stand back up but before I even could get on my two feet, I was knocked down again by another obstacle.

Hit after hit, it became harder to trust the journey. It became harder to try and find hope.

When everything in your life is going okay, and you're knocked down, you have more strength to get back up quicker. But what happens when you are already way down and you get hit again?

It gets harder to find the strength to stand up, to find the hope to not give up, and the willingness to want to even try again.

But when you understand how to rise again and again, no matter how low you are from all the knockdowns, that is when you become *unstoppable*.

You can have the greatest comeback in history when you learn how to commit to the decision that, no matter what, *you will stand back up*.

One way I do this every day is by reminding myself that my fearful thoughts are not who I am. They are a product of my past and I am the conscious being just experiencing them.

....no matter what, you will stand back up

Just because these hardships happened in my past, they do not predict my future. And if I'm still standing after all I've been through, that must mean I can continue to come back from anything.

Another way to be able to have the greatest comeback, is to work to stand up *while* experiencing the knockdown. You don't have to wait until it's over.

Understand that it's okay if you don't have it all figured out just yet. It is okay if you're going through obstacles or tragedies right now as you're reading this. Just because you are dealing with hard stuff that's causing you pain does not mean you can't also bring in the good things, like chasing after your dreams...

Through the seven years of tragedy, I was growing my businesses. I never stopped. My dreams were the light inside all that darkness.

If anyone or anything knocks me down today it may hurt, and it may push me back some; but I can promise you one thing: It will never be able to keep me down.

I'll continue to stand and continue to rise until the day, *I decide* to give up, which will likely never, ever come.

In order to be able to live the life you love, live the life you've dreamt for yourself, all you have to do is keep on getting back up.

Nothing and no one can defeat you without your permission.

Everybody gets knocked down, the question becomes, how quickly are you going to get up?

Action Step: Create your C.O.M.E.B.A.C.K. story using the template below:

Courage- Write down one fear that you must gain the courage to move through, despite the fear.

Ex) I'm afraid I'm going to get sick again. I'm afraid people will judge me.

Opportunity- Discover one opportunity that is available for you today because of where you are.

Ex) I have the opportunity to be able to be near my family. I have the opportunity to start my own business.

Message- Write down the one message you want to share with the world.

Ex) You can always rise from any challenge regardless of circumstances.

Example- What's a personal example of how you learned that lesson/ message?

Ex) Illness, a death, a failure, or getting fired… any specific time in your life where you learned the above message you wrote down.

Backstory- Vulnerably share the backstory of where you were then and how you pushed through to get to where you are today.

Ex) This is where you share more details on what led to you getting knocked down to the point where you discovered the lesson and message.

Action Steps- What are the exact action steps you took during that time?

Ex) I journaled, meditated, registered my business, moved to a new city… What did you do to get through the tough times that others can also do?

Create- What have you created or want to create because of this journey?

Ex) I now live in my dream home; I found my significant other; I started my dream business; I traveled the country. Write out what you created in your life as a direct result of going through the tough times. If you haven't done it yet, this is where you can share what you *want* to create.

Knockdown Repeat- Write down one quote or mantra that will help you repeat this comeback story anytime you get knocked down.

Ex) I trust the journey. I am strong and resilient.

Example of my Comeback Story using the outline provided: I'm still afraid every day I'll get sick, something bad will happen in my family, or my dreams won't work out as I intend but I fear regret more than I fear failure and because of this, I decide to push through. There are so many opportunities that lie ahead for me to share my story and grow my business that I must not give up. I want to show people that regardless of the circumstances they encounter, they have the strength to continue to rise above and achieve their dreams. I know this because I experienced it firsthand. From my near-death experience to my autoimmune disease, I've been knocked down too many times to count, and for a long time I didn't think I'd ever be able to do the things I always dreamt. One day, I decided to stop playing the victim and start taking action. When no one would give me an opportunity to speak and share my story, I created my own stage with my own events. I shared my journey vulnerably every day on social media and I began to take one action step a day to grow my business. I now get to do what I love full-time, I met the person of my dreams, and I'm finally at a point where I'm healthy and happy. It wasn't easy and still isn't, but through this journey I know I will always be able to stand tall after getting knocked down. Every day I remind myself how strong I am and

> *Every day I remind myself how strong I am*

allow myself to surrender to the journey, knowing that everything is going to be okay as long as I never give up.

Once you have your template of your Comeback Story written, you can then elaborate on it. It's important to take the time to write your story out so you have it to come back to when the tough times do come your way. You need to always remind yourself just how strong and resilient you are.

Know that everyone (and I mean everyone) has a Comeback Story and I'm challenging you to discover yours and then share it with others. You never know how your story will change someone's life.

Everyone loves a good underdog story.

CHAPTER TWO

The Bloopers

One of my favorite parts of comedic films are the bloopers at the end. Not only are they hilarious, but also, they make me feel a sense of connection with the actors. It shows their *human side*.

We accept that these actors won't get every line completely correct while filming the movie or TV show. We don't think twice about their Freudian slips or mispronounced names. We just laugh while watching these bloopers and think their mistakes are funny and we laugh even harder if we see them laughing.

While we accept movie and TV bloopers without a question, why don't we accept our own? We hide away in fear of messing up—or worse—being seen *while* we mess up.

But what if we switched our perception of a "mess up" being a bad thing and instead just view it as a blooper? The fact is we're all human and we all mess up throughout our journey, yet we are all walking around trying to put on this show for others in fear of truly being seen. Why is this? Why are we so afraid to mess up in public?

What if we all decided to show up authentically in all areas of our lives? What if we saw our role models, friends, teachers, parents, and colleagues messing up every once in a while? How would that change our level of connection with one another? How would that change how confident we feel when pursuing something new? How much more courage would we have to try something new?

I think people would take bigger risks. I think people would be more willing to chase after bigger dreams or introduce themselves to someone new or audition for their dream role. Whatever it is that people want is often not pursued because of fear of being seen while they are in the growing stages.

But the growing stages are necessary! So instead of "fearing" away from them, we should embrace them because that is the only way to ever truly achieve something.

Whether you are trying to make new friends, wanting to speak up in your next team meeting, or picking up an instrument for the first time to try and learn how to play it, if you allow the fear of messing up stop you, you will always stay in the exact same spot as you are today.

Repetition helps you get better. The more you repeatedly do something, the chances that you'll eventually get it right increases drastically. But that day of you making plans with new friends, leading a team meeting, or playing that instrument in a concert, will never come if you never try.

If you never have that first or second mess up, you will never know.

When I was in high school, I did what most girls did at my school: I tried out for flag football.

I went to a large high school of 3000+ students, and flag football was HUGE.

So big, in fact, that we had freshman, junior varsity, and varsity teams, and still the majority of girls who tried out didn't make any of them.

I went along with my friends and tried out when I was a freshman. The tryouts lasted three days with the third one focused on playing a game of scrimmage so coaches could see us in action.

I was selected to play defensive back.

I stood in position, super nervous, as this was the first time I was actually playing in a game of football. I watched as the quarterback threw the ball towards the wide receiver.

I jumped as high as I could jump (then realized I'm a pretty high jumper) and intercepted the ball!

I landed on the ground, turned around...

...and ran the wrong way!

Before I could hear people on the sidelines screaming "WRONG WAY!" my flags were pulled and that was that.

I was *so embarrassed* I went home crying.

I'll save you from the waterworks of emotions and embarrassment and skip right to the part when the coaches announced who made the team the next day. The announcement was made on a printed piece of paper hung on the coach's classroom door in school.

I waited until people stopped crowding the door so I could look at the freshman team list, hoping that I at least made it to this team.

I held up my pointer finger and scanned the list, my name wasn't there. I was so disappointed as I saw my friends' names on this freshman team list.

Just to check, I scanned the list for junior varsity, yet again my name was nowhere to be found.

Oh well, I guess there's always next year to try out again... even though I knew it wasn't just an *oh well* feeling coming up; I really wanted to be part of a team.

This experience has given me the courage to continue to try new things

My eyes scanned over to the varsity list...

Wait a minute... this must be a mistake... my name was printed on the varsity list!

... I was the only freshman on the team, this *had* to be a mistake I thought.

But no, it was intentional.

After talking with the junior varsity coach who happened to be my science teacher, he said that even though I turned the wrong way, it made me stand out.

The varsity coach continued to ask, "Who was the girl that ran the wrong way?"

It was the mess up, the thing I was so embarrassed about, that led me to making the team!

This experience has given me the courage to continue to try new things, even when I have no clue what I'm doing. Even when I know the outcome may be a bit messy, if I want it, I now go for it. Because let's face it, in life...

You'll never feel 100% ready, so you may as well go for it today.

Doing it messy, allowing for the bloopers, helps you discover your inner potential. It helps you discover something about yourself that you never knew you were capable of.

The coach knew it would be easy to teach me to just run straight the next time I intercepted the ball. What is harder to teach is how to intercept a ball. If I was able to do that without any coaching or practice, how much better do you think I was able to get? He saw my inner potential before I did.

Another thing this experience taught me that has helped me throughout my life and career, is that you must always give it your all, regardless of what others will think.

You can't discover how good you can be if you never fully try. Don't go halfway at something out of fear. Put your entire effort into it as you never know who is watching or what you'll discover about yourself.

I always come back to this story when the nerves set in and I begin to question myself about whether I should go for something.

If you don't feel ready, that's okay. What's not okay is *not* going after something because you don't think you'll be good enough, you don't feel ready enough, or you don't feel it will be "perfect."

Here's the thing about perfection: You'll never achieve it. Because we are our hardest critic and regardless of how "perfect" it is to someone else, in our eyes it could always be better; we could always *do* better.

I'm going to admit something that may shock many of you: I'm a big procrastinator.

Phew, I said it. It's out there.

I procrastinate when it comes to practicing speeches before a big gig, writing a script before I have to film a video (that's why 99.9% of all my videos are improv), packing before a big trip, setting up the lighting and mic before an interview (I literally do this one minute before I'm supposed to go on and I always ask myself why I put this stress on me when I have so much time beforehand). But there you have it, I'm a procrastinator at my core.

I realized recently, I perform the best under pressure, which is probably why I leave everything to the last minute.

But I'm also a perfectionist. I pay attention to details and like to have everything perfect before I launch something to the public.

You can see how these two characteristics mixed can create a ton of stress.

But here's the thing, it has led me to doing things MESSY.

There's no way I can have everything perfect when I only leave a few hours before a deadline to work on a project. With that being said, regardless of whether I gave myself months of time or just days, it would still turn out pretty much the same.

Because the ONLY way to grow is through action. Doing the thing!

So, if you wait and wait until you feel it is perfect, you'll always be waiting because you don't know how to make it "perfect" yet.

Only experience can teach you what to improve on.

I didn't realize that I didn't know which way to start running when I was playing on the defense side in football. But believe me, I will never make that mistake again!

The thing is, you just don't know, what you don't know.

You can do all the research and practice you want, but the only way to truly improve upon a skill or talent is to learn through action.

So, you just need to start. Start messy. Try things out.

Your intentions behind your work are way more important than getting it perfect. If your intentions are in the right place, you can't go wrong.

People love the blooper scenes because they can relate to them. We are all human and we all mess up every now and then. Let's stop hiding away from that and start sharing our bloopers' reel with the world.

There's potential in the unknown, and you should never be in fear of your potential.

Action Step: Think of one thing that you didn't pursue or stopped pursuing because you felt you weren't ready.

Now take some time to complete the following steps:

Step One: Journal this moment out and explain what you believe caused you to feel this way.

Now ask yourself, is this reason enough to *not* go after the things you want in life?

Step Two: Write out one thing you want to achieve today in your life.

Examples:
I want to make new friends.
I want to start public speaking.
I want to find my significant other.

Step Three: After discovering one thing you really want to achieve in your life, write out one action step you can take today, messy or not, that will help get you closer to achieving it.

Examples:
Goal: I want to make new friends.
Action: Sign up for a networking event happening next week.

Goal: I want to start public speaking.
Action: Get on Facebook or Instagram live and talk about a topic of choice.

Goal: I want to meet my significant other.
Action: Sign up for a dating app and ask someone out.

Step Four: Set a date (within the next week) to take the action!

I understand all the above goals and action steps can be scary, because I've been there before.

You may be afraid to meet new friends because the last time you tried you stumbled upon your words, couldn't keep the conversation going, and felt super awkward. Now you're waiting until you feel you are ready to put yourself back out there and have more to talk about with others.

You may be afraid to get on a live stream in fear of messing up in front of others. So, you are waiting until you have the perfect speech and feel more confident.

You may be afraid to ask someone out because you've been rejected before and want to wait until you feel you have the perfect dating profile or picture.

Guess what: You're not the only one who has felt this way! Share your feelings with others and show up even when you don't feel ready. Use this journal exercise to express your feelings and see how much you truly want to achieve the thing you wrote out. Now ask yourself: Are these fears more important than that goal?

You're not the only one who has felt this way!

Remember, people love the bloopers because they can RELATE to them! The more you show up even when you know you may mess up, the closer you'll be to getting the thing you so badly want.

CHAPTER THREE

Be Resourceful

Have you ever looked at someone else's success and thought, *how did they do it?* Then you go into the research bubble and try to reverse engineer how they got to where they are, only to then realize that you don't have everything you need yet to pursue your dream?

You realize there's more to learn. You feel you need more connections. You may even think you need more tools, tech, equipment, or support to be able to do it right.

While you stay in the researching phase, you continue to wait and wait.

You continue to look outside yourself for the answers which only leads to more self-doubt.

You compare your current circumstances to others.

You wish something was different or wish you had more of something or maybe less of something.

The world we live in does this to us.

Knowledge is at our fingertips and while that is an amazing blessing, it also can cause us to go into a state of paralysis.

Constantly feeling like there is some secret to success, feeling happy, or healthy or fit. While there are strategies people have found that can help, there is no secret to getting there.

How do you think these people found this secret you're searching for or that they are selling? They themselves did trial and error! They had to throw a bunch of stuff on the wall to then see what would stick.

Waiting until you have enough money to get the right packaging for your new Etsy store, waiting until you move to that new city to start building meaningful relationships, or waiting until you can travel to be able to learn about new cultures are all excuses! They just delay your dreams and growth.

We live in a world that is constantly changing and with that, we need to be able to keep moving forward through that change. To do that, you need to become extremely *resourceful.*

◆◆◆

It was the summer before senior year of high school, and I was school shopping with my mom. I went into this graphic tee store and spotted on the wall a black t-shirt that had this interesting design on it. It was a hand holding up the peace sign but the palm was the shape of the continent Africa.

The company was OmniPeace and the hangtag shared their mission of ending poverty by 2025. A percentage of proceeds from the shirt went to building schools in Africa, using education to help villages become self-sustainable. I bought the tee (well my mom bought the tee for me) and I rushed home from the mall to head to the family desktop computer to look up the company (the days before smartphones and personal computers).

I went on their website and saw Courtney Cox, Jennifer Aniston, and Zac Efron all sporting the tee I just purchased. I became super interested in learning more about the work they were doing and how I could be part of it.

While exploring the information on their website, I had this crazy idea...

What if I designed jewelry for them?

As someone who was very into fashion (it was my life-long dream to live in New York City and work in the fashion industry), I emailed the company from their contact form and expressed an idea for me to design OmniPeace bracelets to help their mission.

The company at the time only sold t-shirts, a tote bag, and a chocolate bar, so I saw a huge opportunity in the jewelry market.

Summer ended, school started, and I was still checking my email daily only to be disappointed at the empty inbox.

I followed up.

I searched the internet for any other email address I could find other than their website contact form. I emailed those listed on the site.

I followed up again...

and again.

Three months later there it was, an email from OmniPeace!

I had this crazy idea...

The assistant to the founder emailed me saying the founder would like to schedule a conference call with me!

I'd never been on a conference call before and was extremely nervous. I prepared my notes as much as I knew to prepare ahead of time in my journal, went into my dad's office, and got on my first conference call.

I sold her on my idea.

At seventeen years old I became the sole licensee to design jewelry for this L.A.-based fashion company.

To be honest, I didn't even know what *licensee* meant, but learned quickly it meant I could use their logo on my designs and sell jewelry under my own label with a percentage going back to the company and of course, towards their mission of ending poverty in Africa.

It took me about a year to design, manufacture, and produce the bracelets before they were ready to be sold.

I drew up the design ideas in my journal, found a manufacturer through Google, designed the hang tags on a Microsoft Word document (yes, Word!), and got them printed by Office Depot.

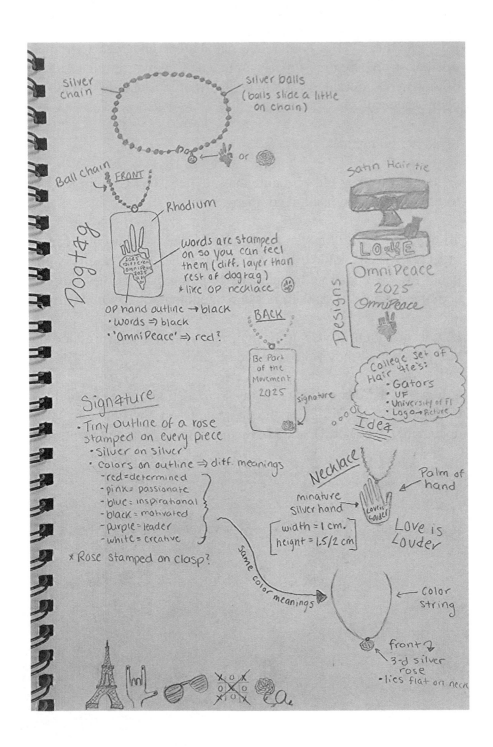

silver chain

silver balls
(balls slide a little on chain)

Dog or

Ball chain → FRONT

Dogtag

Rhodium

words are stamped on so you can feel them (diff. layer than rest of dogtag)
* like OP necklace

OP hand outline → black
• words ⇒ black
• "OmniPeace" ⇒ red?

BACK

Be Part of the Movement 2025

signature

Satin Hair tie

LOVE

Designs

OmniPeace 2025
OmniPeace

College set of Hair tie's:
• Gators
• UF
• University of Fl
• Logo → Picture

Idea

Signature
• Tiny outline of a rose stamped on every piece
  • Silver on silver
  • Colors on outline ⇒ diff. meanings
    - red = determined
    - pink = passionate
    - blue = inspirational
    - black = motivated
    - purple = leader
    - white = creative

* Rose stamped on clasp?

Same color meanings

Necklace

minature silver hand

width = 1 cm.
height = 1.5/2 cm

Palm of hand

Love is Louder

color string

front
3-d silver rose
• lies flat on neck

I need to mention this: I didn't know *how* to do any of this.

I used what I had, and I made it happen. I didn't have tools or financing. No YouTube University. Just sheer desire, the guiding support from my entrepreneurial dad, and a commitment to my goal of selling my jewelry. By the time the bracelets were ready to be sold, I was a few months away from graduating high school, and I sold them the only way I knew how: through word of mouth.

My dad reached out to the local newspaper, and I was written up in the *Palm Beach Post* with the focus on how I was working to end poverty in Africa through my bracelet designs... my first piece of press!

Shortly after, I headed up to Gainesville, FL to start my first semester as a freshman at the University of Florida. I began in the summer and during that semester I was working on selling my bracelets. I quickly learned that word of mouth marketing was not a good strategy. I didn't know a single person on campus and this school had over 60,000 students!

I got my first Mac computer for a graduation present and on it was a free application called iWeb. I began learning how to code a website.

I built my first website and was so excited, yet not one sale came through.

The old saying, "build it and they will come, " is farthest from the truth when it comes to business and sales.

I had to figure out a way to market my website. Facebook was just coming about, and it was more of a social network for your personal life than for business at that time, so I didn't even think of that as an avenue. Instead, I saw how much press the company, OmniPeace was getting and thought to ask the team over there if they could add my bracelets to their website and then when an order came through, I would ship it out.

I had no clue this was a thing called *drop shipping*.

They agreed and my dad helped me set up a PayPal account to process the orders. One day, I came home from class, opened my computer, and had twenty emails from PayPal... twenty sales came in!

Then another and another... I went from zero sales to hundreds within a few weeks!

Every day when I got home from class, I would check on my sales, package them up (using small manila envelopes and my handwriting to write out their addresses), and get on my bike to take them over to the post office.

As the orders continued to roll in, I started to see that I was receiving orders from all over the world, not just the U.S.

I went from zero sales to hundreds within a few weeks!

I began getting orders from Australia, Japan, Canada, Brazil, but there was one problem: My contract with OmniPeace listed my licensed territory as the United States.

I quickly emailed them and expressed how I was receiving orders from people located in other countries and would like to amend the contract.

I still remember, to this day, when I received the new contract from their lawyer showing:

Licensee Territory: ~~The United States~~ The World

This was my first real dive into entrepreneurship (outside of the one-week dog walking business and my handmade denim bedazzled bracelets I sold to my mom's friends), and I fell in love with the process of turning an idea into reality.

·· Adaptable

Through my bracelet business, I ended up donating thousands of dollars to help OmniPeace build schools in Africa and this experience led me to so many extraordinary opportunities. We always seem to connect the dots when looking back; imagine if only we trusted the journey while we were on it!

I constantly think back to this experience when pursuing a new project or goal because I can easily get caught up in the self-doubt, the comparison mindset, or the research bubble, always looking outside of myself for the answers and thinking I don't have what I need to make it happen.

But in order to adapt to change, and not only survive through it but thrive, we must all be resourceful.

Resourceful (adj.): having the ability to find quick and clever ways to overcome difficulties.

An easy way to get into the mindset of being resourceful that has helped me tremendously is to think in common sense terms.

For example, if I asked a group of people of all different ages, to make a toy airplane there would be several different outcomes. Some would go out and buy certain motors and equipment to make a drone type airplane, spending lots of time on YouTube to figure it out and lots of money to make it "right." Most would want to do that but say they don't have the money to be able to make it how they want, so they decide to wait to build it. But there would be one person, most likely a child, who would find a piece of paper, fold it up, and let it glide through the air.

Forget all the bells and whistles and just use what you've got to make it happen!

In order to adapt to change... we must all be resourceful

This is the type of thinking you need to have during change so, no matter what, you can continue moving forward.

Stop making excuses of what you *don't* have and start looking at ways to turn any obstacle into an opportunity to be creative. If you stay on the excuse course, waiting until you have more to pursue a certain action, you'll always find reasons to stop along the way.

Think about the example I just mentioned. What if after you made the toy airplane, I gave you the challenge to sell it. You most likely will respond with another excuse that you can't sell the airplane because you don't know how to build a website or don't have enough money to make cool packaging for your product, and I can go on and on with the list of excuses.

Or you will be resourceful and find a way.

When I was creating my jewelry business with OmniPeace, I did not know how to do any of the things they asked upon those initial conference calls, but I said yes and then I used what I had to make it happen.

Say yes, then figure it out after.

Don't miss out on an opportunity because you think you need more than what you already have. Some of the best inventions, businesses, and movements were created out of nothing, from people who were extremely resourceful.

You have enough knowledge to start.

You have the skills to start.

You have enough money to start.

You have the support to start.

You have the tools to start.

You have what it takes to start.

Action Step: What do you have right now that you can use to take one action step along the path towards your dreams? Think about your dreams and then list out all the resources you have at your use.

Example: computer, cell phone, printer, paper, colored pencils, camera, notebook, library, your parents, a friend, a mentor...

Through this exercise you'll realize just how many resources you do have.

CHAPTER FOUR

The Flexible Plan

We plan, God laughs - Yiddish proverb

Sometimes our plans work out, but sometimes they don't.

The important thing in order to thrive through change has nothing to do with whether or not your plan works out the way you intend; instead, it has everything to do with how you adapt to the changes that come while working through the plan.

All that matters is how you choose to feel, and what you do with those feelings, when things don't go as planned.

Do you feel defeated, or do you feel challenged?

Do you feel like you have failed, or do you feel a sense of adventure of what may lie ahead due to this change?

And more importantly, what do you do with those feelings?

The greatest blessings in my life happened when I followed myintuition, when my plans didn't work out as I intended, and I opened my mind to the signs from the Universe.

What if—just hear me out—we stopped trying to control everything in our lives? Every outcome, every plan, every step along our journey, and we just let it all flow?

Of course, looking back on things after they happened makes it easier to see the blessings that came when the plan didn't work out as intended. When you're in the middle of living through it though, and things aren't going as planned, I understand it is challenging to see the positive.

When I was in high school, I started watching *Project Runway* and it spurred a passion for working in the fashion industry. I was dead set that I was going to be a fashion designer and my parents even got me a sewing machine with a whole sewing table and supplies one year for Christmas.

While I loved designing and drawing, let's just say I didn't have a natural talent for sewing and making clothes. So, by the time I went to college, fashion was still where my heart was for the industry I wanted to work in, I just pivoted from fashion designer to the business and marketing side of fashion.

> *What if—just hear me out—we stopped trying to control everything in our lives?*

My senior year of college, after having just returned from studying fashion abroad in London, my best friend and roommate Angela and I got the opportunity to do social media for a designer during his runway show at New York Fashion Week.

A dream come true!

We flew out from Gainesville, FL to New York City to experience the wonders of being in the city during Fashion Week.

The night before Fashion Week kicked off, they used to have this event called Fashion's Night Out (FNO). It took place in the Lower East Side and every store stayed open late for parties, discounts, and celebrity appearances.

While still back in college planning this trip, Angela and I looked through the FNO website to see what stores had the best parties and giveaways to devise a plan. I decided to create a "FNO Bucket List" so we could hit as many places as possible and create a fun social media campaign for others to follow. (This was during a time I was also working to grow my blog, *Hello Perfect*.)

Bucket List

- Get Christian Siriano's definition of perfect

- Take a picture with Haute Hippie's bedazzled longhorn

- Meet Rachel Zoe

- Get Miss America's definition of perfect

- Introduce ourselves to Daily Candy editors at C. Wonder

- Take a picture with Rev. Run

- Snap a pic at the grand opening of Piperlime

- Get glamourized at Stella McCartney's custom photo booth

- Travel back to London enjoying Fish & Chips at Ted Baker London

- Take a picture in front of every store we visit

- Get Alessandra Ambrosio's definition of perfect

- Decorate a #FNO tote with Honestly WTF founders

- Have #HelloPerfect Fashion's Night Out!!!

Dressed and ready to go with my hot pink, handmade *Hello Perfect* sign, we headed on the subway towards the Lower East Side. The night was young, even though it felt so late to us (we'd been traveling since 3 a.m.). Despite my deliriousness, I was ready to tackle Fashion's Night Out and cross off as many tasks as possible from our bucket list.

The streets were flooded with people like it was the Macy's Thanksgiving Day Parade; I couldn't believe it. There were lines inside and outside almost every store and I quickly realized that there was no way we were going to be able to accomplish everything on our list.

We began taking pictures wherever we could with the *Hello Perfect* sign. I actually got to meet 2014's Miss America winner, Laura Kaeppeler and the Victoria Secret model, Alessandra Ambrosio. When I met each of them, I asked the same question I asked every celebrity I met during this time, "What's your definition of *perfect*?"

Every time I asked, people got so thrown off. I guess it's not such a common question to be asked, but it is a very popular subject. I began asking this question because I hate how people allow society to define perfection for them. In our society, perfection is smooth skin, long hair, a thin body, straight, white teeth, and symmetrical features, but how many of us have that naturally? How many of us actually look like the filters and photoshopped representations that are splattered all over the media?

I hate how people feel bad about themselves because they think they don't live up to this unrealistic idea of perfection. This is also the inspiration behind why I started my blog *Hello Perfect* in 2011.

I was on a mission to redefine perfection and any celebrity that crossed my path would receive that same question and guess what: every single person I've asked had a different answer. So, you see, there is not one set definition for the word *perfect* but rather hundreds of different meanings and it should be unique to you as well.

When I asked Alessandra Ambrosio this question, she said, "Perfect is my kids."

For Laura Kaeppeler her definition of perfect is, "Embracing who you are no matter what you are."

As the night went on, I looked at our bucket list and realized we hadn't even crossed off half! The streets were getting

I was on a mission to redefine perfection

more crowded and I could barely handle fighting my way in between people to get to our next destination just to wait in line.

I felt like I was at Disney World on the busiest day of the year! The crowds were intense from all the lines outside the store funneling up the sidewalks, to the number of people trying to stop you as you passed them so they can hand you a flyer, and to just the high school kids who were out that night and working to make a fashion statement with their appearances and loud banter.

Sounds like fun, right?

I pulled Angela's hand, "Let's go down a side street instead so we don't have to deal with all these people," I said.

She followed me down a deserted street where we stumbled upon polka dotted ladybug beetles (Volkswagen Beetle). They were Marc Jacobs's cars painted red with black polka dots and little wings on the rooftop to promote Marc's new perfume, The Dot.

We saw a few Marc Jacobs male models completely naked, except for tiny boxer shorts, standing around the cars handing out perfume samples. Just a note, at this time, I was still working to learn the skill of confidence. While I normally wouldn't go up to a naked male model, I learned early on while growing this blog that regret sucks. I committed myself to finding the courage to get out of my comfort zone so I would never have to feel that awful feeling of regret by choosing not to do something out of fear.

I asked one of the models if he could hold my *Hello Perfect* sign for a picture after briefly sharing our mission around the blog. I snapped a photo, took back the sign, a perfume sample of course, and was about to go on my way towards our next stop on our bucket list.

The model stopped us and said he heard Marc Jacobs may be stopping by. *No way*, I thought. One, it wasn't on the FNO website that he was participating tonight, and two, it's Marc fu*king Jacobs!!!

I couldn't hear this and leave right away, so Angela and I headed into the Marc Jacobs store which was right in front of where the cars were parked. The store was as big as a regular sized living room. It was tiny, to say the least.

> *I committed myself to finding the courage to get out of my comfort zone*

We made our way over to the drink table and got a glass of champagne. We decided to take one swoop around the store (or try to since there were so many people crammed in that small space), and then we agreed to head out.

"There is no way Marc is coming in this store tonight and even if he was, what are the odds he comes now?" I said to Angela. She totally agreed. Plus, we had so much more to do on our bucket list we couldn't just stand in this tight space and wait all night.

So, we made our rounds and ended up in the back corner of the store by the cash register. Suddenly, it got much tighter. I began to feel like people were pushing me; tons of people were surrounding me. *What the heck is going on?* I thought.

Then I see: Marc Jacobs is standing right *next* to me making his way behind the

> ## *My heart dropped. Genius.*
> ## *Just genius*

counter. *Marc fu*king Jacobs is standing right next to me!* Did I mention he was the first fashion designer I ever loved and one of my favorites still to this day?

I didn't know what to do but then I remembered the *Hello Perfect* sign. Angela was still next to me, and we were both in complete shock. Since everyone was pushing and shoving to get closer to him, I knew this was my chance to ask him my question.

As quickly as he could sign, people were buying his perfume bottles. I realized; this is my ONLY chance. I quickly introduced myself and told him my elevator pitch about *Hello Perfect*. I then asked in a shaky nervous voice, "So… we would love to know… what's your defin… definition of *perfect*?"

Marc stopped signing perfume bottles and looked at me. Without any hesitation—and I mean not one ounce of hesitation—he said, "Perfect, what is?"

My heart dropped. Genius. Just pure genius.

"Would we be able to take a picture with you holding up our sign?" I asked.

Angela and I quickly got next to him on both sides, put up our bright pink *Hello Perfect* sign and I handed my phone to the nearest person to snap a photo. I was starstruck.

People continued to push and it was getting super claustrophobic, so I gave my warmest thanks to Marc and signaled Angela to head out through the swarm of people.

Marc then grabbed my arm. I turned back around pulling Angela back with me. He put his hand down on the counter, and I could see the beautiful cuff s on the well-designed button-down shirt he was wearing. He turned his hand over, wrist facing up, pulled his sleeve up with his other hand and what I saw made my heart stop for a moment.

There, printed permanently in ink on his wrist, a tattoo of the word *perfect*.

I could not believe my eyes. What was I seeing? He had a tattoo of this word? The word that so many people fear yet I created a whole business out of it?

"Can I, um, take a picture of... um... your wrist?"

He obliged. I grabbed my phone and began snapping tons of pics over his wrist as he laid it there on the counter as hundreds of people surrounded us and waited for their turn to talk to him. My hand was shaking uncontrollably. Every picture was coming out so blurry. I was extremely nervous. I finally got my hand steady and snapped one last photo. I think I took like 15, no lie.

I don't know how I worked up this courage (probably was the fear of regret vs. rejection that was pushing me to do what I did next), but instead of just leaving and thanking him for this amazing opportunity, I then had the nerve to ask him if he could hold up his hand next to his head.

He put his hand next to his face and boom, I now have a picture of Marc Jacobs literally saying, *"Hello Perfect!"*

"Thank you so, so much Marc. You made my night!"

After fighting through the crowds, we made it outside the store. Both Angela and I stopped, breathed, and looked at each other. "Did, did that just happen?" I said to her. "I can't even believe what just happened!"

I hugged Angela so tight. Both of us were really at a loss for words.

I couldn't wrap my head around what just happened. What were the chances that we decided to take a back road instead of staying on the main road where Fashion's Night Out was happening...?

... and that we ran into the model who had heard that Marc may make an appearance,
... and that we happened to be in the store when he *did* make an appearance,
... and not just anywhere in the store but right there at the counter next to him as the first person to be able to talk to him!

And besides all of that, he had a tattoo of the word *perfect* on his wrist! Of all the words in all the languages, he was branded with a word that the majority of people stray far from, yet I decided to create a movement around. It all seemed like way too many coincidences to be true.

But then again, I don't believe in coincidences.

It all seemed like way too many coincidences to be true

How can you? Every decision made this night, from all the people pushing us along the main street to lead us to a back road, to the act of courage to talk to the naked male model, to just the tattoo, this is way too much to line up to be a random sequence of events. I believe things happen for a reason and if you allow yourself to be in flow, things align as they should.

We ended the night with five of the thirteen things crossed off on our bucket list. But none of the things we missed even compared to what happened that night.

I had always been a person who maps out and follows a plan. Hence the bucket list for Fashion's Night Out. But my time traveling abroad really changed this part of me. Yeah, I still love writing out a plan on paper (the old-fashioned way) but I've learned that it's okay to diverge from the plan sometimes.

When Angela and I lived in London, we really had no choice but to live spontaneously. It would be Wednesday night and we were done with classes for the week and Angela and I would look at each other while eating chips and dip in our shared kitchen and say, "Barcelona tomorrow?"

Or Amsterdam, Prague, Paris, or whatever other country we wanted to travel to. I would book the hostel; she would book the $30 flight or train (it's crazy how inexpensive it is to travel from country to country once you're already in Europe), and we'd be off the next day with no plan of what to do or where to go.

I would get a map of the city from the hostel we were staying in, since we didn't have a phone for GPS, and just explore, trying hard to read a map that wasn't in English. This way of traveling was different for me, since every time I traveled with family, we always had a plan of what sites to see and where to go each day. But Angela and I were pure wanderers with no plan and no destination in mind.

It's okay to diverge from the plan sometimes

We would walk wherever our intuition led us and stop wherever our hearts desired. This led us to discovering some of the most memorable places: the weirdest young art museum in Prague, a playground with a zipline in the middle of an Amsterdam park, the best pizza we've ever eaten in Paris where we had to wear sparkle top hats that were given to us upon walking in, and now... to meeting Marc Jacobs.

When we are so attached to a plan, we end up losing the magic of the world. We think this plan is the only way to get from point A to point B and if we don't follow it exactly—or if things don't go exactly as planned—it's all a failure.

Yet plans should be flexible. Ideas need to be flexible.

We've seen this with the 2020 pandemic. We have all learned that you can plan all you want but when something tragic hits, those plans go out the window and you must learn to pivot and adapt.

The best way to do this is to be open to synchronicities.

Be open to giving up control of the journey and the outcome. Allow your intuition to guide you to where you are meant to be and most importantly trust that everything will align in your favor.

When hard times hit, allow yourself permission to let plans change, morph, or even let them go. Yes, still create a plan of action when it comes to your career, finances, business, health, etc., but if something happens that throws you off track, be open to the signs that appear. But remember, you must be looking for them!

Don't get so stuck in your head that you are off track because most likely, you are exactly where you are supposed to be.

Surrender to the flow of the Universe.

Action Step: Schedule a day where you get in the car or go for a walk with no destination in mind. The only plan you have is to always turn right and then stop wherever you feel called. Really tap into your intuitive feelings throughout the day, noticing how you feel at certain moments along the journey and where they led you.

Journal the experience. Describe every place or person you encountered and document how each step along the journey made you feel. What did you end up discovering? Who did you end up meeting? What did you learn about yourself?

The purpose of this exercise is to let yourself feel more freedom. When you can give yourself permission to spend a few hours or even one full day living completely in the moment with no plan whatsoever, and making decisions only based upon your feelings, you'll discover what you need to tap into when you are following a plan to achieve your goals. When changes hit and you need to adapt from that plan, you'll have the confidence to know exactly how to do just that.

CHAPTER FIVE

It's Not What, But Who

What do I need to do to be successful?

T his question is one I receive way too often and to be quite honest, it's the wrong question to be asking.

The idea that something outside of yourself will lead you to success is the biggest lie ever told.

Instead of focusing on *what* you have to do, focus on *who* you have to be.

While the strategy is important, it is not the strategy that will lead you to success, it's the person executing that strategy!

It's you!

You are your greatest asset, yet you have been taught to only focus on solutions outside of yourself.

But how good would it feel, how confident would you feel, to know that no matter what path you're on, no matter what changes come your way, you can always find success because you are the one doing the work, because you are the one who has faith in yourself?

◆◆◆

I started Women Empower X (WEX) in 2016 after noticing a big need for diverse women of different ages, backgrounds, and industries to connect and collaborate. I started this business on a whim, from an idea, and a need for community.

I knew there had to be a better way, a more authentic way, to connect with other businesswomen, so I ran with the idea. Basically, I launched it without doing any research around the concept and had no clue if it was being done already (Something they definitely teach you *not* to do when you're in business school).

Since WEX was started off more from this personal need for connection, I didn't have a vision for it at first. I just started it with $2,000 I saved from my previous business ventures and used that as a deposit on the Fort Lauderdale Convention Center to host our first event in hopes I could connect with other entrepreneurs.

I thought maybe 300 people would show up—well I hoped and prayed 300 people would show up—but after seeing how our first event attracted 1,000+ people using only organic marketing tactics, as I didn't have any money to invest in paid advertising, I knew what we were doing was definitely needed.

After experiencing the magic of this community coming together, I started to cast a larger vision for WEX to become a leading company empowering women entrepreneurs and business leaders.

That's when I began to do some research around this idea.

While I started WEX before the "Me Too" movement, the women's march, and the "Time's Up" movement, without my prior knowledge I discovered there are quite a few other companies doing what I wanted to pursue.

These companies had larger budgets, more contacts, and a much larger following on social media than I had.

Right away, the doubt, the fear, and the comparison mindset came flooding in.

I felt so defeated and I was just getting started.

The conversation that ran through my mind constantly for years went something like this,

How can I make WEX a success when so many other companies are focused on empowering women entrepreneurs already?

Who am I to be able to achieve this?

Why would people join WEX when there are so many other companies out there that have larger followings on social media?

During this time, WEX was solely an event company, where we hosted large conferences at convention centers around the country. Before every event, I had so much anxiety wondering if people would show up.

Even as we grew, our marketing budget for these events was minimal, literally I think the most we've ever paid for ads for the events was around $3,000. We were a small company and relied heavily on my speaking anywhere and everywhere to spread the word and organic social media to drive attendance. We also didn't have a budget to bring in large speakers like some of the other companies of the same target audience did.

We attracted thousands and continued to grow, event after event

The doubt and the uncertainty to deliver the audience we promised our exhibitors, drove me to complete burnout.

Yet every event turned out to be a huge success. We attracted thousands and continued to grow, event after event.

But regardless of the success of the previous event, I'd question if we had enough speakers, enough credibility on our stages, enough reach, enough sessions, enough freebies, etc., to be able to drive attendance.

I continued to compare WEX to other events that attracted huge names like the Kardashians or celebrities like Jessica Alba and

Martha Stewart. I knew we couldn't even come close to attracting that talent on our stages due to our minimal to zero-dollar budget and I came super close to giving up because of this.

I came extremely close to calling it quits because of the fear of the competition.

But here is the thing, regardless of who was on our stage, regardless of how many sessions we had, regardless of what food we served, or how much money we spent on ads, people showed up.

And our audience loved it.

We continued to hear the success stories of connections made at WEX. Friendships were created, business partnerships were made, ideas were formed, companies were established... the mission I created WEX on was happening.

During each WEX experience, people came up to me and congratulated me on a successful event. Yet they didn't mention anything about the things I thought we needed in order to make WEX a success. The only two things mentioned was the diversity and the energy.

Not just the diversity on stages but in attendance. We attracted people from all walks of life, all ages, all ethnicities, all industries. And the energy! It was collaborative, inclusive, and welcoming. At WEX people weren't just shaking hands and exchanging business cards, they were sharing not just what they do but *who* they are.

It took me years to realize this but what made WEX a success was the people driving it. Not just me but also our community.

This only can happen though, when you have full faith in yourself.

WEX is a success because of the energy, the mission, and the passion behind why I started the company.

This has been one of the most pivotal lessons I've learned along my journey as an entrepreneur.

No one is you and **that** is your power.

Instead of being so committed to your *plan*, be 100% committed to your *purpose*. And 10,000% committed to adding who you are in what you do.

When you add who you are in what you do, you will always rise above the noise.

Focus less on *what* you need to do and more on *who* you need to be.

The economy can crash. Your business can fail. You can lose your job. You can even lose all your money. But the one thing that can never be taken from you is who you are.

Your personal brand. Your knowledge. Your reputation.

That is what you always have to build upon and that's why it's so important to continually focus on it and feed it to grow.

It doesn't matter if others are doing what you want to do because there is enough room for all of us to be successful!

Stop looking outside of yourself to try and find your point of differentiation in the market,

Your authenticity is your point of differentiation!

Take the time to invest in yourself because you are your greatest asset in life and especially in the pursuit towards your dreams.

Invest in yourself. Invest in continuous education, attending events, networking, coaches, and communities.

Invest in your knowledge and your personal brand.

Regardless of your business, people tend to follow people, not logos.

That's why it's so important to put yourself out there. Especially in times of change.

People didn't come to WEX early on because of the strategy we put in place. They came because I shared my passion for the work we were doing.

Yes, there were other events to attend. Yes, there are still other companies out there focused on empowering women entrepreneurs and business leaders but there is no one like me and because of that, there is never going to be a company like Women Empower X.

You can mimic a strategy but you can't mimic the energy.

The energy around the WEX community is a product of empowering our community to be themselves, to show up authentically, and to help one another get to the next level.

So today while I now do my market research before diving into executing a new project under the WEX brand, I never worry about the competition or let it get to me because I know no one can create like I do.

Understand that you see the world differently than anyone else and when you can create from that place, you will always find a way to be successful.

Be so committed to going *all in* on who you are.

Embrace your authentic you.

Share yourself with the world, vulnerably.

The world needs you.

Action Step: If you removed all of your achievements, relationships, and job roles, how would you describe yourself? Try and write a blurb about yourself without including anything you'd include on your resume. Instead, work to include the moments that *affected* you to the point they changed a part of who you are.

To help, complete the sentences below:

A personal experience that affected me was…

From this personal experience I have…

My example:

A personal experience that affected me was my near-death experience and my autoimmune disease.

From this personal experience I have become a more empathetic person and can share my story vulnerably empowering others to be vulnerable as well. This experience is unique to me and by sharing it, I can help others find strength through darkness and let them know they are not alone.

The purpose of this exercise is to help you discover the things that make you different and unique. These experiences and the person you have become are what will help you stand out from the competition and that is what you must find the courage to share with the world.

CHAPTER SIX

Waiting to Live

I t's easy to make excuses. What's not easy is doing what you've set out to do despite all the excuses you could make.

All the reasons why it's not the right time to…

> … go after your dream
> … start dating again
> … ask for a raise
> … take that vacation

There will always be a reason why you should wait.

I'll make new friends once I move to my new house.
I'll pursue my entrepreneurial goals once I have more knowledge.
I'll be happy when I make more money.
I'll live my life once I overcome this obstacle.
I'll start exercising once I have the right gym equipment.

Sound familiar?

Hate to break it to you, but waiting does nada. All it does is set you back.

Waiting won't make the situation easier, and it won't make you feel more ready.

Regardless of your circumstances, you must always move forward with what you want in this life.

Think about it: You never really know when it all can be taken from you.

◆◆◆

As I lay in bed in the Intensive Care Unit, hooked up to machines that were keeping me alive, I stared out the window and thought...

Oh, how I wish I could feel those sun rays beaming on my skin. How I wish I could run outside right now and have the freedom to drink an iced cold glass of water. I took that world for granted, didn't I?

A question popped into my head that was scarier than the nightmares I was experiencing...

Did I live?

Not *Will I die?*

Did I live my life when I had the opportunity?

I continued asking myself this question over and over again.

This question wasn't asking if I was alive or dead in that hospital bed. The question was:

Did I live my life when I had the opportunity?

I knew the answer was no, but I didn't want to believe it.

What if I am never able to live that life anymore?

I started to reflect upon the things I thought mattered so much, those I'd made into such a big deal, actually didn't matter now that I was lying in the ICU.

I spent so much energy worrying about getting lower than an A on a test, now what did that matter? That A is not going to save my life.

I spent more time trying to get people to follow and like me on social media; now who cares about that? Those likes are not going to save my life nor define my life if this sepsis turns fatal.

I spent so much energy on being depressed about the past. Why did I waste so much of my energy and time on that? Why wasn't I stronger and more resilient?

Why did I wait to live my life?

The last months of my life were in darkness, why? Why would I waste so much time in darkness when there is so much beautiful life out there? WHY, oh God, why?!

I continued to stare outside the window dreaming of the life I wanted to live after college in New York City.

After being hit with some tragic events my senior year of college, I was waiting to graduate and move to New York City to begin my new life and start fresh again, but what if I never make it to New York City?

Why did I wait to live my life?

Why... why... why?

I moved back and forth in my hospital bed trying to ease the pain.

We shouldn't wait until things get better to live our lives, because life can change at any moment. Why did I wait? Why did I take my life for granted? Why did I take water for granted?! Oh man, all I want is a glass of water right now.

I looked around the hospital room, feeling grateful for my friends and family who were by my side.

If I survive, I will live by running through wild fields with the wind blowing through my hair. I won't settle. I won't give into darkness. I will not merely exist, I will fully LIVE.

I've waited for many years… always believing that waiting somehow would make the situation different or easier.

It didn't.

The only thing it did was steal away time.

I risked my life ending while in the waiting zone and I would hate it if you did the same.

It's easy to find the excuse to wait because there will always be a reason to do so. But anything good in life, any big dream or goal you want to achieve, will not be achieved taking the easy way out.

I was waiting for something to change for me to pursue the things I wanted but here's the thing:

You must not wait for your life to change; you must change your own life.

Regardless if you think you are ready or not,
Regardless if you think the timing is right or not,
Regardless if you think you'll be successful at it or not.

No challenge is worth stopping your life and dreams for. Find the opportunity through the obstacle and go after what you want today.

You never know what tomorrow may bring.

Action Step: What is one thing you've been waiting to pursue until you feel you are ready or until something happens? Are you waiting to start your dream business until you have everything figured out? Are you waiting to put yourself back out there in the dating world until you feel you are ready? Are you waiting to post a video on social media until you've had enough practice?

List out the things you are waiting for and be honest with yourself. Also include any obstacles you feel are preventing you from going after something you want.

Example:
- Waiting until I get married
- Waiting until I move
- Waiting until I have more money
- Waiting until I feel better
- Waiting until I meet more friends
- Waiting until I take this course
- Waiting until I can hire a business coach
- Waiting until I have more practice

After you list everything out, take a few moments to reflect over the things you wrote down and for each one, ask yourself, "Is this worth more to me than my dream?" If the answer is no, cross it off and stop letting it hold you back!

Yes, some things would help you achieve something easier but again, anyone can make that excuse because there will always be things or people or resources that can help make things easier. Remember, the person that gets to live the life of their dreams doesn't wait until the easy road is laid out for them, they create it for themselves.

It is as simple as deciding that you no longer will wait, but instead, you will make the decision to chase after your dreams today.

Make the decision.

CHAPTER SEVEN

Focus on the Things you do have Control over

There are a lot of things we cannot control in this world.

Yet we try and try and try.

We give away our energy to all the things we don't have control over.

1. Trying to force an opinion on someone: You don't have control over others' opinions of you.
2. Trying to wish away bad weather when you are planning an event outside: You don't have control over the weather.
3. Trying to control how many people buy your product, book, or service: You don't have any control over others' buying decisions.

What you *do* have control over though is:

1. How you treat others and how you show up every day for them.
2. A backup plan you must create, like getting a tent or indoor venue.
3. Your marketing strategy and sales copy.

There are always solutions to problems, yet too many times we are focusing on all the wrong things, which is the easy route.

It's easy to complain.

It's easy to focus on all the things going wrong.

It's easy to blame situations on outcomes you weren't able to control.

But if you want to be an adaptable leader, a person who thrives through change, an individual who lives up to their fullest potential, you must never take the easy way out!

We only have so much energy in a day to give to others, our work, and ourselves. The more energy you spend focusing on everything you don't have control over, the less energy you have to focus on the things that will move the needle forward.

Not only does this deplete your energy, but by focusing on the things you feel helpless around, it also decreases your level of confidence!

And that is something we must never do.

◆◆◆

When I was in the Intensive Care Unit, struggling to survive from sepsis, I was in a lot of pain, to say the least.

I was out of the coma at this point, yet still very much in the *danger zone*. I still had a mask on my face, a tube down my throat, and I was hooked up to nine different bags of antibiotics. I couldn't move, breathe, or speak on my own, but I did have control over my thoughts.

When there is physical pain in your body it's very difficult to focus on anything other than that pain. It takes over your mind like when a dark cloud blocks the rays of the sun.

Sitting in that hospital bed day in and day out I knew that if I continued to focus on the pain, it would never cease to exist. What you focus on is what you manifest so I knew I needed to redirect my thoughts to something more positive.

During this time, I felt the only thing that would make me feel better was a glass of iced cold water, but of course I couldn't have that since there was this tube down my throat and the doctors said I wasn't allowed any liquids.

When I closed my eyes, I envisioned this glass of water.

I saw myself running on my high school track. I don't know why I was on my high school track as I never ran track before (I did try out but didn't make the team).

But there I was running, around and around this track. The track was bright orange, a little bouncy and the lanes looked like they were newly-painted as they were perfectly filled in with white paint.

It wasn't too hot outside and it was just me, alone on this track. It was quiet. I was running and running to try and make it to the finish line.

I could see the finish line from a distance as I came around the last turn. It was just a straight sprint ahead until I made it.

At the finish line I saw my mom, dad, and sister. I saw my best friends. I saw my old teachers and mentors. I saw friends from my sorority and some of my aunts and cousins.

They were all waving at me and cheering me on. It was still silent though. There was no noise. Silently I saw them cheering and I then spotted a

> *When I closed my eyes, I envisioned this glass of water*

GIANT glass of iced cold water. This glass had to be about three feet tall. My mom and dad were holding it together ready to pour it all over me and into my mouth.

Oh man, I couldn't wait any longer. I ran faster and faster as I wanted that giant cup of iced cold water to stream down my face and into my mouth!

I was running but my family and friends weren't getting closer. I couldn't move past the spot I was currently at, but I kept running. I was not about to give up.

Water at the end of the race.

Water at the end of the race.

Water at the end of the race.

I kept saying these words in my head. Over and over again.

As I focused on these words and this vision that I wanted so badly to manifest into reality, my pain dissipated. There was no room for negative painful thoughts in my mind as it was overtaken by my visualizing, with positive words and feelings, towards getting to the finish line.

While I didn't have control over any of my bodily movements, including my breathing, I did have control over my mind, and this alone I believe, saved my life.

This experience led me to learning one of the greatest lessons along my journey and that is this:

You must focus on the things you do have control over.

Don't give away your energy to the negative. Don't give away your energy towards things that won't help you move forward. Protect your energy at all costs.

Next time you are having thoughts that cause you to feel a bit low, a bit helpless, and maybe even bring on some self-doubt, catch yourself in those feelings. Notice them. Then ask yourself if you can control this.

If not, move on. You're wasting precious time and energy.

If there is something in your control, redirect your thoughts towards that.

Today, every time I feel stress around my business, and find myself focusing on all the things I don't have control over, like others' actions, whether or not they will buy from me, show up, engage, etc., I catch myself in the act of these thoughts and choose to redirect them towards what I *can* control.

I choose to focus on things like our marketing efforts, how I am showing up as a leader, and the investment into my education to grow my knowledge.

Throughout your journey there will be many times you waste energy on things you can't control; it's our human nature. But the key here is recognizing those thoughts and redirecting them as soon as you do notice them.

Not only will this help you protect your energy and achieve more along your journey, but it will also help you enjoy the process regardless of the changes you must adapt to along the way.

Life's not about learning to find your inner power. It's about learning to use it.

Action Step: Focus on the goal you are working to achieve. Now, write in your journal anything you are currently worried about regarding that goal.

For example:

- I'm worried people won't show up to my event.
- What if people judge me when I'm speaking on stage?
- What happens if I mess up?
- I hope they choose me.
- I wonder what the other candidates are like.
- I hope they like me.

Now go through the list you just wrote and ask yourself for each item, "Do I have any control over this?" If the answer is yes, take action. If the answer is no, work to find something you *can* control that will help relieve you of this worry.

For example, from the list above:

- I'm worried people won't show up to my event.
  - I can't control if people show up or not. I can't force them to come.
  - I can control our marketing efforts and our sales copy. Let me spend time re-working our marketing strategy to find what is giving us the highest return on our investment so we can double our energy there.
- What if people judge me when I'm speaking on stage?
  - I can't control others' opinions of me.
  - I can control how much I prepare ahead of time and my level of confidence when I'm on stage.

Repeat this exercise for every thought that comes to mind while working towards any of your goals, both personal and professional. Not only will it help raise your confidence level and decrease your self-doubt, but it will also help move you towards taking the right action steps to get closer to achieving your goal.

CHAPTER EIGHT

Unrealistic Reality

When change comes it's a bit scary, but when it stays it's terrifying.

They say the only constant in life is change, and life has certainly proven that to be true for me. While I embrace change and most of the time really enjoy the adventure it brings on this journey, when the change is so big that I feel out of place, it can be overwhelmingly hard to stay strong.

Have you ever randomly found yourself living your life but you felt like you were out of your own body? Like you were looking down at yourself wondering who that person was… like you were in an unrealistic reality?

It doesn't feel familiar to you and the life you know, and all of a sudden here you are living this brand-new life and it strikes you all at once: a feeling of uncertainty, fear, and of not just feeling out of place but more like an out of body experience.

People fear big change because they don't know what they don't know; the uncertainty is so powerful that they stay in the same life, doing the same old routine day in and day out.

Coming from someone who has experienced big change and this feeling of fear more than once, I now understand truly why people stay stuck or stay in a life they've always lived, never venturing out.

It's very scary!

But I will say this: I'm still here.

And while not all the change I experienced brought joy and happiness, it brought growth and adventure. Sure, some adventures were scarier than others, but today I can honestly say every single one was well worth it.

◆◆◆

The first time I experienced this out of body feeling of "What the heck am I doing with my life?" was when I went to study abroad in London as a junior in college at twenty years old.

The first month or so I was immersed in the experience of being abroad, studying fashion in London, and traveling Europe with my best friend on the weekends. But then after a month or so, I remember going for a walk and just getting hit like a ton of bricks with this overwhelming feeling of fear. This feeling didn't hit *me* though, it was like I was watching myself from out of my body and that's when I saw and felt the fear.

I felt so out of place; I didn't know what I was doing there for a moment and questioned who I was becoming and the life I was living far away from the place I knew as home.

Maybe it was a strong feeling of being homesick as that was the longest time I had gone without seeing family, and being unable to talk or facetime with them every day was super hard for me.

But whatever it was, the entire experience in Europe felt like I was living this *unrealistic reality*.

> *Maybe it was a strong feeling of being homesick*

The days were filled with my spending a few hours in class learning fashion with students from all over the world who spoke all different languages or checking out the local fashion street markets or booking a cheap flight and hostel with my best friend to go explore another country in Europe.

This life was so foreign, not just the food and the people, but the way I was living.

I grew up in the suburbs of Boca Raton, Florida. I was always close to family, always did what I was told, and always followed the rules.

While in London, all of that went out the window.

I was super adventurous, and perhaps not as smart as I should have been when it came to my safety. I found my way into the top clubs and pubs of London partying with some of the richest people in Europe. I went to new countries without any plan or knowledge of what I was going to do there. I made out with guys after just meeting them at a pub. I rode the tube to get to and from class. Angela and I ordered pitchers of Sex on the Beach at this weird old movie theater-turned-bar and met random people on a Wednesday afternoon. I drank in the middle of the day (as that's definitely the norm in Europe) and I lived my life in this unrealistic reality.

It was amazing and scary all at the same time, but this change in pace and lifestyle was definitely out of place for me. There were days when I was alone walking the streets when it would all hit me at once, and I'd question myself, "What am I doing here? Who is this I'm becoming? What is this life I'm living?!"

A journal excerpt I wrote during this time that maybe can explain these feelings a bit better.

The definition of reality is the state or quality of being real. This reality that society has normalized has put limits on the achievements our creative minds can accomplish. Your conscious mind creates your reality, so why shouldn't your reality be what you want it to be? This girl is a helpless dreamer living in an unrealistic reality. While she is growing up, she remains young at heart searching for her dreams in this world. Normality is something she stays far from and daydreaming is a common activity. She is still on the path of finding herself while realizing that her true happiness remains in her utopian dreamland. Once she figures out how to break away from society's reality she can fly away to her conscious Neverland.

The next time this feeling of living in an unrealistic reality came was during another big change I went through following college graduation, post-near-death experience, when I moved to live in New York City alone at twenty-one years old.

This no longer was a summer internship stay. It was permanent and I was away from everyone I loved.

During this time, I was getting sick again from what I didn't know yet was the onset of my autoimmune disease. This life I was living included waking up super early to workout in my apartment building, walking the busy city streets to get to Time, Inc. where I never felt fashionable enough walking through those doors, spending the day working in a cubicle at *InStyle* magazine, and at night, making dinner and working on my blog. During the weekends I'd walk miles through the city, many times spending my days in Central Park (before it was too cold).

In the beginning, I loved it. It was everything I had been dreaming of since I was ten years old. But after the months went on, I'd started to feel that wave of "What am I doing here?"

Was this the life I wanted to live for the rest of my life? Did I always want to be a plane ride away from my family? Was I ever going to be able to make friends or meet people here? Is this who I am or is this who I thought I wanted to be?

I was entirely free from everyone and everything yet I felt so chained down in my pain of uncertainty with my health challenges and the post-traumatic stress I was dealing with following my near-death experience. These chains around my heart got tighter and tighter each day living in New York City, causing me to feel like I lost who I was.

What am I doing with my life?

I was numb to everything. Once again, I felt like I was living in an unrealistic reality. But this time, it was one I most definitely did not want to be in.

Another time I experienced these strong, scary feelings was later when I decided to leave South Florida, move all my stuff to Dallas, Texas in my parents' house (which was completely foreign to me as they just moved there a year prior after living in South Florida my entire life), and travel the country speaking as much as possible.

I left the life I knew back in South Florida because after my parents left, and I didn't have much family there, I didn't see why I was staying. I was living alone, traveling a lot, and while the place felt familiar because it's where I grew up, it no longer felt like my home.

After moving to Dallas and spending every week in at least one hotel room and on multiple planes, the fear of this unrealistic reality, of "What am I doing with my life?" started to rise.

There I was, going back and forth from Dallas, a place I definitely didn't feel like was my home, and I was traveling the country by myself. While I loved what I was doing, I didn't feel aligned with where I was headed on this path.

Is this the life I wanted for myself or am I just trying to run away from things?

If I'm being completely honest, I was trying to run from everything. Running from health challenges, from a breakup with a good friend of mine and business partner, from my parents' own challenges, from everything.

I was running and this hit me like a ton of bricks each time I got on another plane, looked out the window, and felt like I once again, lost myself.

> *I am here to follow my heart, even if it leads me to pain sometimes*

These feelings are no longer foreign to me, I know them all too well with all the change and tragedy that's come my way. While I only share the change above, each experience included its own set of challenges and obstacles… as well as achievements and amazing memories.

They all brought about both hard times and good times, and they were drastically on opposite ends. The hard times were extremely challenging, and the good times were a feeling of euphoria I never once experienced living in the routine "safe" life. But that's why most stay in the same environment they've always been in, around the same people they've always known, doing the same thing day in and day out. Because it's safer.

And it is.

But I wasn't put here on this planet to live a safe life.

I am here to follow my heart, even if it leads me to pain sometimes.

And while the pain is hard, it's worth it because the good moments are unlike anything you can possibly experience living a "safe" life.

In the Spring of 2019, only six months after I moved to Texas, my family decided to move to Raleigh, North Carolina to follow my little sister to North Carolina State University College of Veterinary Medicine.

We'd all been separated for so long, the job my dad got in Texas didn't work out, and my sister was the only one who truly had to be in a certain location, so we all moved with her.

After this move, I got hit hard. Yet again.

We were living in a hotel room for a little over a week until my parents closed on our house and the day after we moved in, I had to take a flight back to Dallas just to get my Remicade infusion (the medicine I have to inject in my body for the rest of my life as a result of my autoimmune disease) since I didn't have insurance or a doctor yet in North Carolina.

Sitting there, in the infusion center surrounded by older people getting infusions, I just started to cry. This was my reality: to have to fly alone somewhere just to get medicine and sit here with this drug pumping through my veins for three hours. I usually am super positive when it comes to this, but I was exhausted, I felt out of place, I felt like so much change just occurred in the past six months; I didn't even know what time zone I was in.

During those months of not really having a home base I traveled to fourteen different cities for speaking, business, and like I said, I was just running away from life.

And now here I was, in Texas getting an infusion.

I slept on my friend's couch that night and flew back to Raleigh the next morning.

Then the out-of-body experience—seeing myself live a life that I thought didn't belong to me, didn't feel right to me or familiar— took over.

I started to get sick. I lost my voice for a long period of time and for a public speaker getting ready to host one of our largest conferences for Women Empower X in Washington D.C., it was too much.

I lost it to the point where I couldn't even talk to sponsors and speakers on the phone.

I didn't slow down though; I was hustling a mile a minute to keep up with my business and pushing all these feelings I had aside. My mom, dad, and sister would go exploring Raleigh on fun bike rides through all the beautiful parks there and I was stuck at home, too sick to ride a bike or even go for a walk.

Again.

Always too sick to do what I wanted... This was my new reality, but it was no longer new to me. I had been experiencing this now for six years.

I moved back in with my parents when we all moved to Raleigh together, and after having finally gotten healthy enough to be on my own a year prior, I felt like I was just moving backwards. And once again, I was victimized by my health.

I cried every day during the first few months in North Carolina. I felt so out of place; I didn't know what I was doing there other than being close to my family.

There I was, a Jewish city girl who always had a dream of living in the big city now living in North Carolina.

I tried to take a mindfulness break one day during work (I work from home) to just breathe in nature and I put on my rollerblades and skated up my parents' street where we lived.

My sister went with me and rode slowly next to me on her bike. When we turned around and headed back to my parents' home, my speed started to pick up.

We lived on a steep hill that I never noticed, being so in my own head and feelings, I guess. Suddenly, I started going faster and faster.

> *This was my new reality, but it was no longer new to me*

I had been skating my whole life in South Florida, so I knew how to slow down but there was no slowing down with this momentum; I was gliding, and I had no way to stop.

This was my wake-up call. I, again, saw myself in this unrealistic reality

We don't have hills in South Florida so this was definitely unfamiliar to me.

I was going faster and faster down this hill, heading straight to our cul-de-sac, and the only options I had were to crash into the neighbor's house in front of me or slide into the grass.

I slid into the grass and the entire left side of my body (I, of course, was wearing shorts) got scraped up. I walked inside my house with my sister yelling for my dad; I wasn't in too much pain but then all of a sudden, the white spots of light started to appear in my mind.

Blackout.

I woke up on the couch with ice all over my legs.

This was my wake-up call. I, again, saw myself in this unrealistic reality.

I was moving way too fast, trying to keep up with my business and the life I *thought* I was supposed to be living and I wasn't slowing down to take a breath or take care of myself, pushing away the hard feelings and fighting against them.

The Universe was telling me to slow down by taking my voice away from me and by my getting sick, but it took a literal crash while moving way too fast to finally see the life and path I was forcing myself to be on, and to finally recognize all the signs from the Universe.

I learned this the hard way. It took a lot of pain, suffering, illness, and literal knock downs to realize I needed to stop fighting what was and allow what I wanted to flow in.

I realized the more you fight for or against something, the more suffering you feel. When you allow yourself to surrender to what is (that does not mean give up or give in, there's a BIG difference), the growth comes and while the pain may still be there, it's different from suffering because you know there are better days ahead.

You know with all your might, that these experiences are necessary.

Loving what is, frees your soul. It allows you to be present and to feel and experience and share it all with others. It allows you to not feel so alone.

After these experiences living in North Carolina for a few months, I shared what I was going through with a good friend of mine, Debra. I shared openly about the feelings of being set back since I'd moved back home with my parents and in this foreign city.

She pointed out something that was so eye-opening for me.

> *You know with all your might, that these experiences are necessary*

She said every time I've ever moved back home, since college, was because I was sick.

She was right. I always moved back home when I was too sick to live on my own and there I was, back home, and I got sick right away. I was resisting and fighting against this current reality of living back with my parents, only viewing it as a bad thing because of my past.

Because after five years of being a victim to my autoimmune disease, I was finally healthy and on the track of growing my dreams and moving forward with my life when I moved to my own apartment in South Florida and my parents moved to Texas.

A year and a half later I found myself back in with my parents and this felt like everything was once again just taken from me.

But that was farthest from the truth.

Sometimes you have to take a step backwards in order to take the right step forwards.

As I write this, it's been two years living in Raleigh and I'm no longer living with my parents. I'm healthy and living in a house I bought with my soon-to-be husband. And my parents, thankfully, live ten minutes down the road. My sister still lives with them while in vet school. We are all here, finally close to one another and all healthy, each of us overcoming our own tragedies we've experienced the last eight years.

It's something I'm eternally grateful for every single day.

But here's the thing... I still feel like I'm living an unrealistic reality.

I still have days when I look at my life, like I'm the outsider looking in, and don't recognize the life I'm living.

But what I've realized along this journey is that any big change, both good and bad, will bring about an unfamiliar feeling.

Right now, it's my first time living with a guy and I'm moving to the next stage of my life. That's an amazing thing but that doesn't mean it feels comfortable. It feels extremely uncomfortable because it's new! But that doesn't mean it's not right.

All big change brings discomfort, but through that you must turn back to your heart to know if it's a *good* discomfort. If it's not, you may find yourself on a path that is not aligned with the life you want to live.

The feelings I had in NYC or traveling alone without any home base or any way to feel grounded were not right for me. And that's why there was so much unbearable pain that was attached to each experience.

But the unrealistic reality I'm living today doesn't include any pain. Sure, it's scary. It's still super unfamiliar. I still feel like I don't belong in North Carolina, and some hardships come with that, but that's far different from intense emotional pain.

If I'd always stayed in my small little bubble, in a life I was familiar with growing up, I'd never have gotten to where I am today nor where I am headed.

I truly believe that.

It's comforting staying in the same hometown your entire life, never venturing to meet new friends, or always doing the same thing day in and day out. That's the easy way to live your life.

But you are here for a bigger reason. And whether you've been on that course for sixty years or twenty, there is always time to step into the scary uncomfortable feelings to discover something deep within you: the person you were always meant to become.

Sometimes life changes you, and sometimes you decide to change yourself. The key is to keep going.

To truly discover your fullest potential, to truly live fully while you have time here, you must be brave enough to step out of the routine once in a while, to explore new territory, to meet new people, and to be uncomfortable in your own life so you can discover your true purpose.

You can settle for what you think is the best it can be, or you can gain the courage to explore everything this world has to offer, everything *you* have to offer this world.

What you think you know is the key indicator of everything you truly don't know.

If you feel like you're living a foreign life—a life that doesn't feel familiar to you because you moved out of your hometown or you're far from the people you love or you just quit the job you had for years to pursue your own business—know that it will all be okay as long as you never give up on yourself.

Tune into your heart; know that the hard feelings of "this doesn't feel right" are okay to have if you know deep down you made this change for a reason.

You are strong enough to get through it. You will adapt. Live through the unrealistic realities of life with an open mind and an open heart and it will always lead you to where you are meant to be.

Action Step: Think back to a time when you felt like you were moving backwards, away from your dream reality. Write down that moment in your journal. Following that time/moment/experience, what followed that turned out to be a blessing?

Did you meet a mentor, a new friend, or fall into a cool job opportunity? Did you pivot or pursue something you didn't think you would? Write down each major experience/step that happened due directly to the previous step. Start to connect the dots that led you to something positive in your life today.

Can you see how every step connects to the next one? Even if you felt you were moving forward or backwards, they all connect and that in itself should give you the confidence to know, no matter what unrealistic reality you're struggling in right now, it will lead you to a beautiful moment or experience, as long as you never give up.

Keep connecting the dots.

Moving home from NYC + leaving my dream city + career in Fashion

- Started public speaking + sharing my story in South FL

Noticed a need for diverse women to connect + Founded Women Empower X

Grew my Personal brand, got signed by a speaking agent + connected with my community.

Grew WEX to 4 cities + at an event connected with Publisher who I then signed with to get Adaptable published!

CHAPTER NINE

Plan Q

Let's be real, if your plan A always works out, you're not dreaming big enough nor taking enough risks. Plan A doesn't always work out. Plan B doesn't always work out. Plan C doesn't always work out. Who cares what letter of the alphabet you're on, as long as you are still trying! Throughout your life, you'll change. Through that change, you must adapt. You sometimes have to pivot. And many times, you have to experience failure, obstacles, tragedy, and challenges that you'll have to overcome. But regardless of the experiences that change your life, if you never give up, you will get there.

I believe that to my core. 100%.

If you never give up, you *will* achieve what you are meant to achieve.

If you never give up, you *will* accomplish your dreams.

It may look different from what you envision for yourself, but in the end, it'll all make sense.

Do not give up. Create plan after plan after plan.

I'm not sharing this out of thin air; literally, I'm on Plan Q in the pursuit towards my dreams!

◆◆◆

PLAN A: I started my first (real) business when I was seventeen years old designing jewelry for an L.A.-based fashion company.

I sold out of my first run of bracelets. I designed a necklace and guess what, I still have 50% of inventory left.

PLAN B: When I was nineteen, I started a blog called *Hello Perfect* with the mission to instill confidence in girls and young women. In the early stages, the blog was focused on fashion, mainly because I wanted to work in the fashion industry.

The blog started to grow and then I alone couldn't keep up with writing for it while still in school, so I brought on several interns to contribute to the blog.

PLAN C: My friend Angela started working with me on it and we turned it from a fashion blog to a healthy media site. Basically, we were trying to be the *Huffington Post* of good news.

PLAN D: Trying to scale from just a blog to a media site, we got a radio gig and started *Hello Perfect Radio*. It only lasted a few months because we then traveled to London to study abroad and the internet wasn't able to support a US-based radio show in our small dorm room from London.

PLAN E: After London we saw how much social media was growing and started another business as a social media agency called A. Rose Media (both our names start with A and we happen to both have the middle name Rose).

We got one client and we were working to close on another client, a designer in the fashion industry. We even flew to NYC to meet with him in person. Unfortunately, it didn't work out. For one, I had no clue how to sell at this time or even position our agency for success. In addition, I wasn't super passionate about doing social media for others, I just always wanted to be working on my own brand with my blog.

PLAN F: After graduation I moved to New York City and was working for *InStyle* magazine while keeping *Hello Perfect* as my side hustle. This was only a few months after my near-death experience, and during the early months living there alone, I started to get sick again. This is when I was diagnosed with my autoimmune disease.

Shortly after I received the diagnosis, I enrolled into the Institute of Integrative Nutrition which was an online certification program to become a Certified Holistic Health Coach. I did this to learn about how to heal my own body with food and of course, being the entrepreneur I am, I had to create a business out of what I was going to learn.

I became a Certified Holistic Health Coach after investing thousands into the program and a year of studying, and let's just say, I didn't end up getting any clients for this new health coaching business of mine.

But what the program did do was lead me to becoming vegan and gluten-free, as I learned how to use food to heal my body.

PLAN G: After about a year of living in NYC, and falling more ill, I made the hard decision to move back to South Florida to gain the support of my family. (NYC is not the best place to live when you're sick.)

Still working on *Hello Perfect*, I couldn't turn a profit for the life of me. I hated working on the website and I just wanted to create, inspire, and one day have my own *Hello Perfect* talk show.

That's when I had this epiphany, *Why am I trying to build a healthy media site when I continue telling myself I hate working on the website and can't wait for someone to take it over?*

** Always recognize signs from your intuition for keys to getting back into alignment with your purpose.

That's when I turned the blog into a 501(c)3 registered non-profit.

PLAN H: There were many periods during this time when I had flare ups with my autoimmune disease that would last months. I went in and out of doctors' offices and hospitals to try and discover something that would heal me, trying to find a mix of medicine and food that would make me feel better.

It was really difficult to find food I could digest and what was even more difficult was figuring out how to cook these types of meals all alone, especially when weak and sick. My mom decided to go vegan so she could support me on my journey. She and I juiced every single day, took wheatgrass shots, and cooked up all different foods.

We basically took my favorite foods and just replaced ingredients with vegan and gluten-free alternatives. These meals turned out so beautiful that I began taking photos and posting them online. People would ask for the recipe and that's when I decided to write my first book called *The Simple Gluten-Free Vegan Cookbook!*

My mom and I created the meals, I wrote down the recipes and took all the photos. Then I found a freelancer online to create the book layout for me, got an ISBN number, found a local publisher that had a self-publishing division to print my books, googled how to put them on Amazon and bam, I was an author!

PLAN I: Not knowing how to mix this new health and wellness focus with *Hello Perfect*, which was now a non-profit (Hello Perfect Foundation) in addition to the blog, focused on confidence and anti-bullying, I separated the two and registered another business under Alexa Carlin LLC.

I was now growing my personal brand as a leader in the health and wellness space as well as working on *Hello Perfect* as my non-profit.

PLAN J: I started teaching cooking lessons at Whole Foods (did you know they have a classroom you can ask to use for free?!) and I hosted some meditation classes at a local yoga studio splitting the ticket profits with them.

When I was well enough to speak publicly, I sold my book at a table and signed copies afterwards. While I sold out many times, as I grew as a speaker, the cookbook wasn't the thing people wanted. They wanted a book about my story. They wanted the lessons; they wanted tapes of my teachings so they could share with others.

I realized at this moment that healthy food isn't where my genius zone was, it was in the motivational space.

PLAN K: The app Periscope was just launching, and I jumped on it early. I started a livestream show on Periscope called *Morning Motivation with Alexa.* I hosted this every morning Monday through Friday and the longer I did it, the more my audience grew. I started having thousands of people who would tune in live to my show!

My personal brand was growing and I was working to become an *influencer*.

I created a community to stay connected to my followers, sold bracelets that acted as a motivational reminder to not give up, launched a Periscope online course to teach others how to grow a following, and even started getting booked for some speaking gigs to talk about social media marketing.

But as a first-time influencer, I said yes to every barter deal versus asking for money. So, let's just say I had a ton of products from a range of companies I didn't need, and still no cash flow outside of some bracelet and online program sales.

PLAN L: Remember that Certified Health Coach certificate I got? Well, I now knew how to make it useful. People in my audience continued to ask for my advice around business and marketing so I used what I learned from this program regarding how to run a coaching business and I started taking on a few business coaching clients.

While I enjoyed this, it wasn't something I wanted to do long-term. I always knew deep down that my way of making a difference is not through one to one, but one to many.

PLAN M: I started to invest more time into my speaking career and when I would reach out to organizations to speak on my story, and no one gave me a shot, I decided to start hosting my own local events. (*When no one gives you a stage, create your own.*)

The events I started to host served as fundraising for *Hello Perfect* and the foundation, but I was only charging about $10 to attend and I partnered with local businesses so I could host my event in their location for free in exchange for promoting their business.

The events began to grow, and it went from event #1 attracting five people in attendance to event #4 attracting fifty people.

While I was now growing as a public speaker, and raising awareness for *Hello Perfect*, I still wasn't making enough money to *not* work another job. I was still playing it small.

PLAN N: A friend of mine started hosting yoga events at the convention

> *When no one gives you a stage, create your own*

center and he asked me if I ever thought about doing my smaller events for women on a larger scale. My wheels started turning and I came up with the idea for Women Empower Expo (WEX), an event that would solve the problem I continued to see amongst women while I was speaking at events... an event focused on collaboration over competition.

An event that not only attracted millennials or women of a certain background but ALL women. An event focused on diversity and inclusion bridging together women from all backgrounds, all ages, all ethnicities, and all industries.

He introduced me to his contact at the convention center, I registered for a new business, and we were off.

PLAN O: While growing Women Empower Expo for the first year, I still had *Hello Perfect*. Yet, *Hello Perfect* wasn't making money and I also felt way less passionate about it.

I was building out programs in middle schools to teach anti-bullying and help them increase their self-esteem. I hosted DreamCatcher Wall events (a concept I made up while in college) in the courtyards of middle and high schools to empower students to write down their dreams and "catch" them on the wall.

This was all through money we raised being a non-profit since the schools didn't have funds to support this kind of training. I was working endless hours trying to raise money while also creating the non-profit initiatives to get into schools, all by myself. Every weekend I'd set up a booth at a farmers market to raise money and try to get supporters.

After a while asking for donations and creating programs in schools, I realized it just wasn't for me. One, I felt that I wasn't the right person to teach about anti-bullying. Two, I hated, with a passion, the fundraising aspect of running a non-profit. Three, intuitively it just didn't feel right and I knew this was not where I was meant to be.

When I started *Hello Perfect* (the blog) back in 2011, I thought this would be my business and career for the rest of my life. I had big dreams and goals. I have tons of notebooks with idea after idea for

·· Adaptable

the business. But experiences changed me and this no longer felt aligned with who I was.

I decided to close the business.

It was an extremely hard decision to make—I think the hardest one yet along my entrepreneurial journey—to close the business, and really, this chapter altogether. At first, I felt like I failed. But I now can see how I *had* to go through all of that to get here.

Without *Hello Perfect* in its many iterations, there would be no WEX. Without the early *Hello Perfect* I would've never been learning social media when it first started to get popular, thereby getting ahead of the curve. There is so much I learned from this venture.

Hello Perfect was taking up most of my time and I knew that if I wanted to make Women Empower Expo a success, I had to give my 100% attention and energy to it.

PLAN P: Women Empower Expo initially started as an expo to connect diverse women covering a wide range of topics from yoga classes to chiropractic care to motherhood. After the first Women Empower Expo in October 2016, I started to shift WEX towards a focus more on the business side of being a female entrepreneur. So instead of a yoga class, we'd have a speaker talk on how to start a business in the yoga industry or instead of general motherhood tips, we had a panel on balancing a business while being a mom.

After we hosted five events, three in Fort Lauderdale, and two in Washington D.C., we pivoted towards not just being an expo but a full-on immersive experience and changed our name from Women Empower Expo to Women Empower X, the "X" representing *experience*.

PLAN Q: The 2020 pandemic hit and in-person events and speaking engagements were no longer a viable option. I looked at my goals and dreams I've had on the backburner and moved forward with the one I already was planning on pursuing, yet never had the time while running three large WEX conferences per year.

We pivoted with purpose and launched the WEX Membership—an inclusive online membership community for women to gain the education, connection, and access to take their business and brand to the next level while being part of a supportive community of women from all walks of life.

We provide our members with coaching, done-for-you templates, and access to experts to help members beat overwhelm by delivering everything they need to know in an efficient, concise manner so they can focus on the right things that will help them grow. We work to connect our members with opportunities and the right stakeholders as I believe you are just one connection, opportunity, or decision away from possibly transforming your entire life, and we want to deliver that one thing to you.

This membership community is stage one of many new initiatives to come around WEX and my personal brand so I'm sure by the time this book is in your hands, you'll be able to see a few more letters added to my pivot list.

I've pivoted A LOT along my journey. One thing with pivoting though, in order to feel you are making the right move, you have to do it *intentionally*.

> *I believe you are just one connection, opportunity, or decision away from possibly transforming your entire life*

You never want to pivot just because of outside circumstances or because you feel like you failed. Instead, you want to see each pivot as a step along your journey getting you closer to where you are meant to be.

Every step backwards helps you discover the right step forward.

Nothing you do is a waste of time, energy, or money when it comes to your dreams and growth.

You have to go through the experience in order to get to the next level. You learn something from it. You gain something from it. It becomes part of who you are and that is what will help you achieve what you want.

As you can see, I've had a ton of different plans along my journey and if I stayed stuck on one or felt because my Plan A or B or even C didn't work out or that I should just give up, I wouldn't be here writing this book for you.

Who cares what plan you're on? Who cares how many times you have pivoted? Keep on dreaming. Keep on taking action steps. And always remember *why* you are doing what you are doing.

While my paths changed over time, my mission has always been the same: **to make a difference, each day, in at least one person's life.**

So, whether I was doing that through bracelets, a blog, a radio show, a non-profit, an event, or an online business, I was still staying true to my core mission.

That's how you pivot with purpose. Stay true to who you are, what your bigger vision is, and what fills you with joy.

Don't be stuck on the path, plan, or strategy because there is not just one right way to make it happen.

There are a million different ways to get to where you want to be. Don't **EVER** give up after the first try.

Action Step: Write out your journey like I did above, with each new venture being the next plan. See what letter you are now on. Now look back at each step... Do you see any connections? Do you see how one step was needed in order to get to the next one, even if they are completely different ideas, plans, or jobs?

Now that you see you've pivoted before, likely many times before, don't you think you can pivot again... and again? It's no longer that scary seeing how you've already done it numerous times in your life and career.

* I'd love to know what letter you're currently on! Share it with me on social media, tag @AlexaRoseCarlin.

CHAPTER TEN

K.I.S.

We make things way more complicated than they have to be. Or at least I do. Take, for example, conversations, relationships, and careers.

Conversations- I read way too much into them.

Relationships- Expectations make everything more complicated.

Career- I have to do everything under the sun to keep up...

or at least I used to think this and it led me straight to burnout.

I do believe most people, myself included, make things way more complicated than they need to be.

And when you do this, you lead yourself right to overwhelm and exhaustion.

When you are working to adapt in new environments, and learning to rise above obstacles, the number one thing that will keep you stuck is complexity.

If something is too complex, too complicated, or you're trying to do everything yourself, it's going to be extremely hard to be able to adapt quickly enough or thrive through the changes.

You will stay stuck, because it's nearly impossible for anyone to grow in that type of environment.

I'm speaking from experience here. I learned this while growing WEX. I was making everything way more complicated than it needed to be. And I mean *everything* from our marketing strategy to project management to our sales workflow. I went way overboard on it all because I thought that's what it took.

No, I was 100% wrong!

Through all the changes and pivots I've experienced, I'll share that the only way to truly become adaptable to lead yourself (and your team) to the level of success you desire, is through simple action.

Simple.

But how do we simplify our life and our business or career?

As I like to say, "K.I.S. the model."

K.I.S.- Keep It Simple.

◆◆◆

When I started to make my first hires at WEX it was very hard for me to delegate things and try to let go of control. I am a Type A personality but when you're also an entrepreneur, your business feels like your whole heart and giving someone the reins to make decisions or complete certain tasks that will directly affect the business is super challenging.

As a result of this fight with myself, I ended up making things way more complicated than they needed to be. I knew I was doing way too much and I knew I needed to delegate certain tasks away from my never-ending to-do list, yet I felt I couldn't let anything go.

I wanted everything anyone did to be written out multiple times so I could see it on our project management software, on our customer relationship manager, and sent to me via email. I needed to make sure each item was documented in all the places so I could ensure

I had to really take a step back and think

it was done correctly and I would be able to find it easily.

I thought this was the right move but what ended up happening was my team spent more time writing updates in all our different software and less time selling or marketing the business.

When our sales team couldn't keep up with the administrative tasks that went along with each sales activity, because I made it way more complicated than it needed to be, I ended up having to take it on so they could be out there actually selling.

This cycle, embarrassingly, lasted for a while until I saw my team couldn't keep up with the growth of the company and our inefficient systems.

This was a super challenging time in my business because it led me to coming close to giving up. When your team is maxed out on their level of energy and time and you yourself are already burnt out, what do you do?

I had to really take a step back and think about what needed to change if I wanted to make WEX a sustainable business.

I knew I had to change everything in order to make it simpler for my team while also seamless for growth.

I started with the first sector of our business that was extremely overwhelming for all of us: marketing.

I took out a big white board and began writing out everything we were doing to market the business. And I mean *everything*.

For example, instead of just writing out Instagram, I'd write out Instagram stories, posts, reels, IGTV, and live-streaming. I continued writing every single item we did for our marketing efforts on this white board, took a step back, and was overwhelmed just looking at the board.

Wow, I thought, no wonder we are overwhelmed!

What I did next was measure each activity by analyzing the data, trying to really understand our return on investment for each activity. (Defining investment as time, money, staff, and energy.)

From the results, I began to cross off every item that didn't produce a high ROI (return on investment).

For example, Instagram stories were working great for us, IGTV, not so much- *delete!*

The result of this exercise led me to creating one of our strongest marketing strategies yet and it saved my team and me hours of time, stress, and overwhelm!

I continued doing this exercise for each sector of the business, simplifying each process as much as possible.

After this year of simplifying my business, we had our biggest year yet

To make it fun I would say to myself while working on this solo in my apartment at the time, "Time to K.I.S. the next model!"

This helped me really understand how to manage a growing business with a small team and little resources. It also led me to create standard operating procedures for every process so then as I began to hire more people, I didn't have to feel overwhelmed training them. I had systems, where each process was laid out step-by-step and they had everything they needed to just follow and implement.

After this year of simplifying my business, we had our biggest year yet, and we had the same resources and team as the year prior!

Many times, it's not that we need more help or more resources to turn something into a success but rather we just need to shift the *way* we are doing things.

I know I make things way more complicated than they need to be. I do this not only in my business but my personal life as well.

I used to stress myself out with all of the things I thought I had to do when really if you focus on the few tasks that actually matter, you'll achieve a lot more and be able to actually enjoy the process.

I K.I.S. everything now!

Every strategy in my business, every decision I make in my own household from interior design to planning family gatherings, to even my own style, and the way I dress.

Simple for me has been a game changer because it has allowed me to persevere and eliminate so much overwhelm.

Life is complicated as it is, and especially when you are hit with a huge change you aren't familiar with. If you try to solve it with more complex solutions, you're going to find yourself in a rut or worse, burnt out.

Simplify the process.

Simplify your actions. Simplify your decision-making process. Eliminate the unnecessary so you can make room for every new opportunity.

K.I.S. the model.

Action Step: How can you simplify your life and career right now? For example, in your business/ career, are you seeing results from being on every social media platform under the sun or can you just focus on two? How can you K.I.S. your marketing strategy so it's more effective and less complicated? What things are you engaged in that are stealing excess energy? What could you let go of or remove from your life to make it simpler?

Start with a brain dump. Choose one area of your work or your life where you feel overwhelmed and begin to write out *everything* you are doing around that. Then, take some time to measure the results of each activity. If the return doesn't outweigh the level of investment you're putting into it, remove it!

You can work through this exercise for every area of your personal and professional life, from keeping your house organized and clean to searching for a new job. The more you can simplify each area of your life, the more time and energy you will have to focus on the things that matter, and the more time you'll have to enjoy the process.

CHAPTER ELEVEN

Hearing all the Sounds

Meditation for me is a tricky thing.

Everyone wants to tell you to meditate but their solution of how to get the running stream of thoughts out of your head doesn't always work, at least not for me.

Let the thoughts just pass.

Envision a streaming light going down from the sky to the top of your head and flood through your body.

Focus on your breathing.

Yes, some of those techniques have worked for me while sitting and meditating in solitude, listening to an audio recording. The problem was, they didn't work when I needed it most: through my daily activities.

When I lived in New York City, I'd take the subway everywhere. The summer prior, before my near-death experience, I'd fit into the native NYC-look (listening to headphones or reading a book while commuting on the subway). However, this chapter of my life in NYC was different.

Every time I put my headphones on to listen to music, even when it was happy music, I'd end up crying. Every time I tried to read a book, I'd read a full page without comprehending one thing (hopefully you aren't doing that with this book 😌). I just read because I couldn't get out of my thoughts.

I needed to calm my mind and meditate during this time, but I was too afraid to just close my eyes while sitting on the subway alone, as that isn't the safest thing to do in NYC. So, all the meditation techniques I was learning weren't a solution.

I would try every day to hold back the tears, but the waterworks always found their way out.

If I tried to just sit there with no music, podcast, meditation, or book, I'd cry. I was in such a dark, lonely, scared place that even when I tried not to think about anything, the memory of my physical trauma produced tears of fear and heartbreak.

One day, while sitting on the subway, I decided to redirect my thoughts towards something else, something in the *present* moment.

I challenged myself to try and hear as many unique sounds as possible.

The sounds started…

The rolling wheels on the tracks.

The music that's too loud from someone else's headphones.

The intercom speaker voice saying what stop we just arrived at.

The shuffling of the kid's feet next to me.

Someone coughing.

A group of friends talking.

A page from a book being flipped.

There were always more sounds to be heard. I tried to listen to them all at once and determine how many different sounds there were.

Suddenly, we arrived at my subway stop.

I walked off the subway and realized, for the first time in a long time, I had made the whole commute without crying!

the beautiful and transformational practice of mindfulness

I didn't even think about my past, my current challenges, or the things I feared. Nada!

I was completely immersed in the present moment.

Wow… this is what it's supposed to feel like, I thought.

If you try and listen to as many different sounds as possible the next time you're in a noisy restaurant or environment, see how hard it is. It's nearly impossible to hear every single one of them uniquely as opposed to all the sounds mixed together into noise.

But as you try to sift them out and truly listen, you'll find that in order to do that successfully, you must be fully in the present moment. You can't think about all the stuff that's going wrong in your life or the fear you have around the future. If you allow all the space in your mind to be filled with those thoughts of your past, current, or future challenges, it would be impossible to hear the sounds.

You must be fully in the present moment and what I learned from this experience, is the present moment is where all peace lives.

At the time I was confusing meditation and mindfulness to be the same thing, thinking the only way to achieve peace was to close my eyes and visualize myself being someplace else. When really, what I discovered at this time was the beautiful and transformational practice of mindfulness.

Mindfulness is a practice of being in the present moment, without getting caught up in past or future stories.

You can do that while brushing your teeth, taking a shower, walking down a street, or being in a noisy subway.

You can do that without listening to soft music, without closing your eyes, and without sitting in a certain position. There are so many different styles, traditions, and practices of meditation and mindfulness and enormous benefits around each of them, but the key here is to find what works best for *you*.

When you're going through challenging times, do not box yourself in with others' solutions or even with your own previous solution. Each experience along your journey may require a different approach, and that's okay!

What I see happening a lot when it comes to mediation, yoga, exercise, and self-care is that when the solution from the experts doesn't work, we never question the solution but instead question ourselves.

We think we are doing something wrong, that we are the damaged ones, or that we are too broken if something doesn't provide the results people promise.

Every single person in this world is a unique being and with that, your experiences are unique to you, your perception of life is unique to you, and what you need to heal will also be unique to you.

If you've tried everything under the sun to heal during times of tragedy, trauma, intense change, or while going through a difficult obstacle, yet nothing has really helped the way you need, try something new.

Make it up! There are no rules here!

Follow your intuition and do what **feels** right to you. Not what you think is right. What **feels** right. If you turn to **yourself**, you'll always find the right **answer.**

Action Step: Next time you are in a busy place, try noticing your different senses. Pick one sense and then try to discern the different things your sense is picking up.

For example, imagine you are at a busy restaurant.

Hearing: how many sounds can you hear? Do you hear the waiter talking to the table next to you? The iPad the little boy is watching at the table behind you? How about the chef yelling out an order or the door opening and closing?

Sight: How many colors can you see? Do you see the light shining through the glass window while also seeing the white apron the waiter is wearing? How many colors can you count within your view?

Smell: How many different scents can you smell? Can you smell the wine you're drinking while at the same time smell the warm bread in the basket and the steaming soup passing you by that the waiter is taking to another table?

Touch: Can you discern the different sensations on your body? Can you feel your butt on the chair, your napkin lying flat on your lap, and your fingers holding the cold silver metal fork? Can you feel your hair touching your ears and the ring around your finger?

Taste: How many different flavors can you taste? Are you able to taste the sweetness of your wine, the butter in your potatoes, and the garlic on your vegetables?

When you are not in the present moment, you won't notice many, if any, of the above senses. However, when you are fully immersed in the present moment, you can in any moment, decide to recognize all of them.

This practice is a sure-fire way to get your mind back in the present moment instantly, in any environment, under any circumstance.

To go a step further, create a journal entry for each sense you focused on and try to list out every single thing you heard, saw, smelled, touched, and tasted.

CHAPTER TWELVE

Will you let it?

How many times have you heard the saying, "What doesn't kill you makes you stronger"?

Do you believe that?

Really, deep down to your core, do you believe that saying is true?

I believed it was true until I experienced something that almost *did* kill me and for years it in no way made me stronger. If anything, it made me so weak and frail I could barely stand on my own.

◆◆◆

There was one time while living in New York City after my near-death experience and struggling with what would become the onset of my autoimmune disease that my friends tried to pick up my spirits by taking me out to a Gator bar to watch the University of Florida game with other Floridians.

I was making my way through the crowded bar, not drinking anything other than water, and I remember that suddenly, a rush of weakness came over me. This feeling of weakness was one I had never experienced before.

Suddenly, my heart started to race and I felt myself beginning to faint.

This wasn't the type of fainting where I went unconscious for a moment, this was just pure weakness. My body wasn't even strong enough to hold me up.

Here's where I began to have a thing against the saying, *what doesn't kill you makes you stronger,* because people would say it to me and I didn't believe it. I felt my near-death experience caused me anything but feeling stronger.

It left me on my bathroom floor for years huddled in a fetal position, too sick and weak to get up. It left me stuck in hospitals and doctor offices crying to them when explaining how nothing was working. It left me alone, with only my mom, dad, and sister left by my side as everyone continued with their own lives. It left me with no energy, not able to digest any food for years, and struggling to keep any weight on.

My near-death experience that did not kill me most definitely did not make me stronger.

It took me years of dealing with more tragedy to realize something about this statement so many have spoken before. This saying can actually be very true, but only if it includes four more words I believe are missing.

What doesn't kill you makes you stronger… *if you let it.*

The more you get knocked down and the more you decide to stand up, you'll realize it is not the experience, the tragedy, the hardship, or obstacle that made you stronger, it is *you.*

You are the one deciding to stand back up every single time you get knocked down. The moment you give up, the moment you decide to lay there on the floor and give into circumstance is the moment you'll realize this saying, "what doesn't kill you makes you stronger" is no longer true for you.

YOU are the one that gets to decide if experiences will make you stronger. You are the one who decides if you will have the grit to keep going.

You are the one who ultimately decides how the story of your life will unfold.

So please never forget,

What doesn't kill you makes you stronger... if you let it.

Action Step: If you are breathing right now, that means you conquered everything from your past and you are still here, alive. Whether you are still working through past struggles or hardships, you're here and that is something to be extremely grateful for. That means you are strong enough to keep going. Strong enough to let the past make you stronger.

So right now, the action step is to make a simple decision and declare that decision by writing it down in your journal. Decide that you will embrace your hardships and allow them to help you grow. From here on out they will not hinder you or pull you back, the only thing they will continue to do is show you just how strong you really are. Because if you are breathing, you beat them. You won. Keep going. Just decide.

Write this in your journal in pen, big, and bold. Feel free to change or add anything as you write it which feels right to you. Let your heart do the talking.

I have decided that my obstacles and hardships are part of me, but they will not define what I can or cannot do. I have decided to let my challenges make me stronger. I am, and will always be, strong enough to continue to stand back up after getting knocked down. I will not let anything or anyone keep me down, that I know for sure.

Sign the bottom of the page where you wrote this.

If you want to even be bolder, snap a photo of it and post it on social media! *(Tag me so I can repost and cheer you on! @AlexaRoseCarlin)*

CHAPTER THIRTEEN

Find the Good

As a leader, innovator, entrepreneur, go-getter, change-maker... it is your job to FIND THE GOOD.

Too many people are reacting to life versus leading it.

We react to everything that is happening around us and we wait until the good finds us in order to be happy.

But being adaptable is not about sitting in the backseat hoping and praying one day things will change for the better, it's about creating that change for the better.

The quickest way to adapt to change and create the life you want is to always search for the good.

Find the opportunity through the obstacle.

Shine your light through the darkness.

Find the good through the most difficult times.

Regardless of how challenging life may seem, there is always some good to be found.

But it is *you* who must discover it.

◆◆◆

It was eight or so months living in NYC since I moved there after my college graduation and all the excitement of my future ahead quickly went out the window with the onset of more illness and suffering.

Most of the days during that time in my life are a blur, living more in my head than in any sort of reality, but there is one moment that I remember so vividly still to this day.

I was suffering from post-traumatic stress and every time my heart beat a little fast, I went into panic mode that something bad was happening. I feared everything in my body: every feeling, sensation, and even thought.

I was in my room with the door closed, in the apartment I shared with Angela and another roommate, lying on my bed crying—a thing I did often during this time—and I remember feeling so much loss of hope. At this time, I didn't know I had an autoimmune disease; I just knew I couldn't heal from my past trauma and my body was definitely telling me something wasn't right.

I was doing a lot of healing work during this time to try and push through these hard days, from reading books by spiritual leaders to listening to guided meditation tracks. Every single book, practice, or spiritual leader had something in common: They mentioned focusing on gratitude. I remember lying in my bed trying to think of what I was grateful for.

I couldn't find one thing.

Was I grateful for my dreams? They led me to be far from my family in order to pursue them.

Was I grateful I survived sepsis? It led me to this suffering.

I remember so vividly still to this day

Was I grateful to be living in NYC? I'm far away from everyone I love.

Was I grateful for my family? They aren't here right now for me.

There is always something to be grateful for

When you are so stuck in darkness it's really challenging to find anything to be grateful for because you are in so much pain it's almost impossible to see your way out from the negative waves clouding your judgement.

But I remember this moment lying in my bed, so stuck in my head and the pain and fear that came every time I felt my heart beat a little quicker, when a loud siren from down below on the city streets went off that brought me back to my present state.

I remember looking straight ahead at my toes, I wiggled them, and I wrote down in my journal: I am grateful I can wiggle my toes.

There is always something to be grateful for, which means there is always some good to be found, but you must work hard to seek it out.

You must do this not only when you're going through a hard time, but every single day. Because let's face it, most of the time things don't go as planned. Most of the time, the things we are planning are not based on our own actions but the actions of others or things out of our control.

When we allow those things to affect our internal state, we are saying those external things are more important than us.

Now, of course things will affect you and not everything is your fault. I certainly do not believe it is my fault that bacteria got into my bloodstream and left me in a coma fighting for my life or that I have an autoimmune disease.

I can't completely fix it or get rid of it, but I *can* find the good through it.

There are three ways to help you discover the good:

1. Remove all expectations
2. Stop comparing your life to others
3. Always focus on gratitude

When you do all three above, you'll be able to remove the blocks standing in the way of you discovering the good.

That is what makes a person *unstoppable*.

They can adapt to anything thrown their way because they will always be successful at finding the good, seeing the light, and helping others do the same along the way.

Here's a perfect example of how your life will pan out when you choose to let everything externally affect you.

You are scrolling through social media and see people traveling to amazing destinations. You see photos of clear blue skies, a couple having a romantic picnic, someone decorating their house beautifully for fall, a perfect family portrait on someone's porch... you see all of these images and then the expectations and comparison mindset rolls in.

Now, you try to emulate one of these photos you saw, expecting that it SHOULD be the same experience for you.

Imagine this scenario...

You book a vacation at a beach resort only to find it is raining two out of the three days you are there. You try to take that photo on the beach like you saw on Instagram the one day it's not raining but the lighting is horrible, the wind is blowing your hair in your face and the person you are with is complaining about having to take so many photos of you. (Yes, this is a true story. Still trying to get Colby to enjoy taking photos.) And of course, your bathing suit is not even close to being as cute as the one on social media.

You look back at your photos compared to the ones you saw, and not only do you feel disappointed from your experience during this vacation since it was raining most of the time, but you also now feel bad about yourself!

The harsh self-doubt starts to creep in and now you are replacing confidence with self-doubt and your actions and life will look completely different when you allow this to happen.

What if though, instead of feeling disappointed, sad, or frustrated with your vacation experience, you challenged yourself to find the good during these three days?

Think of it like a scavenger hunt and you are on the lookout for the good.

Day one that it's raining, you start exploring the hotel inside and discover a hidden wine cellar you can take a tour of. You follow where the good takes you and end up having a super cool experience on this hidden wine tour.

Day two, you ask the concierge what there is to do when it's raining, and they share one of the best local restaurants in

> *Think of it like a scavenger hunt and you are on the lookout for the good*

town and offer a free shuttle there and back. You arrive and there's live music and dancing and not to mention, the best tacos you've ever tasted!

Day three, you enjoy the beach since it's not raining anymore, and you take that photo you've been wanting. You laugh as the wind blows in your face and realize it would be a lot better to just have the hotel in the background instead of the beach so your hair won't be in your face. When you look back in the photos, you realize how beautiful the sun is over the hotel and it reminds you of this perfect vacation you just had.

The only reason it was perfect was because YOU made it perfect.

Stop wasting your days wishing the day looked different.

Stop wasting your energy feeling disappointed.

Stop wasting this period of your life feeling sorry about what happened or what didn't get to happen.

It's okay to have some expectations and it's okay to want certain experiences, but just know what they are. Know that no matter what happens, you will make it a great day because you can.

Your challenge in life, from here on out, is to find the good in every situation.

See if you can live up to this challenge.

It's not an easy challenge and there will most definitely be days you don't live up to it, but if you can try each day to find the good, your life will be a whole lot more fun.

The key is to not wait until life forces you to change, but rather lead your own life so you choose how you want to adapt to experiences.

I've found the good in my darkness and yes, sometimes darkness wins the fight, but my light will always win the war.

Action Step: Challenge yourself to find the good today and every day. Throughout the week, go on a scavenger hunt for the good and document in your journal everything you found. Mention every experience you shifted from a negative one to a positive one and every unexpected, good thing you discovered.

Example of my journal entry:

Scavenger Hunt for The Good

- There was no coffee this morning because we ran out and initially, I found myself getting super annoyed and starting off my day on the wrong note. I decided to just do a quick run to Starbucks and ended up getting a free coffee because the person in front of me paid it forward! I then paid for the person next in line and I immediately found the good in these random acts of kindness!

- I was heading to a meeting and running a bit behind, already somewhat stressed and so I decided to try and calm myself by putting on some music. My Bluetooth for some reason was not syncing to my car and I became so frustrated I just put on the radio. I took a deep breath and the song that came on was "Wonderwall" which is one that brings back so many amazing memories of my trip in Europe with my best friend Angela. Immediately I found the good in having to turn on the radio because my Bluetooth was not working.

- My friend cancelled plans on me for the weekend which I was really looking forward to. A few hours later I got a call from my speaking agent for a last minute virtual paid speaking gig. Because my friend cancelled, I was able to take the gig- found the good!

·· Adaptable

CHAPTER FOURTEEN

Surrender

The world is filled with people who love to try and control everything.

Now I'm not saying that's a bad thing; we care about certain things happening in our life and so we try to control the journey to make them happen.

When students want to get into a certain college, they get stressed when the timing comes for acceptance letters to go out. They hope they did everything they could between all the late-night studying, extra-curricular activities, and the endless volunteer hours and more, to get into the school of their choice.

Some parents even get stressed around this time too.

If the students get into the college they want, along with what their parents want for them, all is good in the world.

But if students don't get into their dream college, parents start calling the admission offices, the students start to feel bad about themselves, defeated, and the experience of going to college is now different.

Instead of it being one of the most exciting times, it's a reminder of how you didn't get accepted to the school of your dreams because in your mind, you weren't good enough.

We try to make what naturally didn't happen, happen

Fast forward to adulthood and those feelings may carry over. Like, for example, when you interview for your dream job and the position goes to someone else, when you run for office and don't get elected, when you start a business and your competition gets all your dream clients, or when you post on social media and only three people like it.

All of these experiences, big or small, make you feel like you aren't good enough and not only that, but you now also believe you are on the wrong path towards your goals and dreams.

Society makes us believe that if we don't get what we want *now*, it will never happen.

If you don't get into your dream Ivy League school, you won't be as successful.

If you don't get *this* specific job, it will be hard to climb the corporate ladder.

If your business isn't producing cash flow, it never will.

Here's where we try to control the situation at hand. We try to make what naturally didn't happen, happen.

It's the same with relationships. How many times have you seen a relationship where one partner isn't happy and wants to break up but the other partner won't let them? They do everything in their power to make sure that doesn't happen, even when they know deep down, it's not working out. This is different from fighting for love and fighting for the people you love. This is when you both know the relationship is over but that reality of being on your own is just too hard to imagine so you do everything in your power to stay together.

All of these are examples of you trying to control your life.

You are working against the Universe.

And that is exactly why people say, "Life is hard."

Life is amazing and wonderful. Life is filled with magic and wonder. Life is beautiful.

But many times, we make it harder for ourselves. Don't get me wrong, I'm completely guilty of this as well.

◆◆◆

When I was living in New York City after college graduation, I was working a dream job at *InStyle* magazine. Yet after a few months there, and falling sicker to what I didn't know at the time was the onset of an autoimmune disease, I didn't feel happy.

I didn't have the energy and excitement I had the summer prior while working in fashion, living in the city.

Maybe it was because my entire life changed between the last time I lived in the city and after my near-death experience. Maybe it was because I missed my family terribly. Maybe it was because I was getting sicker and sicker and was suffering from severe post-traumatic stress disorder.

It could have been several reasons, but all I knew was that I was not happy working at what I thought was my dream job.

I tried every day to perceive it differently but I knew deep down, my experiences—the tragic events that occurred that year prior—changed me.

I remember going to Central Park on the weekends and just sitting on one of the grass hills looking at a beautiful view, watching couples, friends, and families having picnics and laughing together. I was so alone. I felt so alone, and I would sit there trying to hold back the tears as I wrote in my journal. I could never hold back the tears so I would just try and hide them away from anyone who looked over at me. But who was I kidding? I was invisible in the city.

I journaled and journaled. Trying to figure out my feelings.

One journal entry I wrote while sitting in Central Park...

9/15/2013

"When you laugh, the world laughs with you. When you cry, you cry alone."

My mom continues to tell me this quote and she couldn't be more spot on. I don't blame anyone for me being lonely. Who wants to hang out with someone who is sad all the time?

But it is hard to just flip a switch on my feelings. While I am getting better (hopefully) I still am scared out of my mind.

Scared of what may be wrong with me.

Scared of my health issues.

Scared of my career.

Scared of living away from home.

I just don't know what to do because I don't have the answer to any of those thoughts. Also, I'm not happy at work. It's just not meaningful to me and I feel I am wasting my time a lot of the days. I feel I should be doing more. Making more of a difference. Doing something I love.

So yeah, uncertainty in everything can make you depressed. I know I will get out of it; I just don't know when. I've been sad for way, way too long. This diary was started to help me sort through all my feelings last December and now I'm still writing about sad things ten months later!

I'm so over it!

I NEED to make a change. A big change. I need to figure out what will make me happy. I need to re-find my purpose. I need to find myself again.

Like my mom just told me on the phone, "You used to have an aura about you that when someone walked into the room, it felt like sunshine."

Used to, key words.

I need to get that aura back.

Being a Type A person, I try to control everything, including my feelings. I was trying to force this life to be mine. Trying to force myself to be happy in NYC even though I knew deep down it wasn't right for me... *anymore*.

It used to be, and I used to feel so at home there. I used to feel connected there. I used to know that was my place. But after everything that transpired, I changed. And my desire changed.

It used to be, and I used to feel so at home there

Four months after this journal entry, I was worse. I'd find myself coming out of the gastroenterologist's office, walking down an empty alleyway, and just collapsing against a building ending up with my arms wrapped around my legs crying into them while crouched on the sidewalk. People would pass but I didn't care. I didn't notice them and they didn't notice me.

I was empty inside. I was beaten down. I had lost hope.

During this time, I lived in midtown west which was just steps away from Times Square. But when you live in NYC, you avoid Times Square at all costs. Way too many tourists and people who walk slowly and don't understand the city.

But one evening, I just was fed up with feeling sad and staying in, so I decided to take a walk by myself with no destination in mind, and I found myself headed towards Times Square.

I was walking with my head down, way too much in my head. *Always in my head.*

And as tourists started to bump my shoulder on each side with every step I took, I looked up from my feet. There it was, all the lights on the buildings, all the people, the energy of Times Square. And at that moment I felt a huge weight come off my shoulders.

The first time I traveled to New York City was when I was ten years old, my mom took me there right after 9-11, and I vividly remember seeing Times Square and just feeling so alive, so amazed this was a place people lived. From that very moment it was my dream to live there.

While looking up and walking through Times Square, I remembered that feeling my ten-year-old self had and all of a sudden, I felt lighter. I was no longer thinking about the past or my current reality of hard feelings, I was completely immersed into the present moment.

I surrendered to this moment, not trying to control the crowds, my thoughts, my feelings, or even where I was headed. I just surrendered.

As I continued to look up and walk forward through the massive crowds, I spotted something on the sidewalk ahead of me. It was money. I looked around and no one was standing by it, everyone was just moving so fast in either direction not paying me any attention.

I bent down and picked it up, it was a $5 bill faced up.

Upon picking it up, I felt a feeling I've never had before. A huge wave of relief like God was telling me, *Everything is going to be okay. Just trust me.*

At that moment I had the realization that changed the course of my life.

I was trying to force my old life into my new reality.

I was trying to control my feelings and intuition because I thought they were wrong. For many years, I believed this was my dream!

But everything was showing me otherwise. I was in complete resistance to my feelings, to the signs, to this life, and it was causing me so much pain and illness.

At this moment I realized that while I was passionate about the fashion industry and this used to be what I envisioned

> *At that moment I had the realization that changed the course of my life*

my life to look like, this dream didn't belong to me anymore.

It was meant for someone other than me.

That moment, the chains that were so tightly wrapped around my heart, slightly loosened.

This is just one experience of the power of surrendering, of eliminating resistance in life. But this story is not finished yet...

Fast forward to a few weeks later: I was leaving NYC and moving back home to my parents' house in South Florida. I needed their support as I was becoming sicker and sicker with my autoimmune disease, and I realized that this NYC fashion dream no longer belonged to me.

It was one of the most difficult decisions. I blamed my near-death experience and my autoimmune disease for a very long time, that they were the reason all my dreams were taken from me. But *that* Alexa didn't fully understand the power of surrendering yet.

Now living in South Florida, I spent my days with my mom going in and out of doctor appointments trying to find something that would heal me. I went to every doctor under the sun, eastern medicine, western medicine, integrative, holistic... and every single doctor had a completely different solution.

I was listening to all of them; I was a victim and I just wanted someone to help save me.

I was a victim and I just wanted someone to help save me

At one point I was not allowed to eat the following foods: meat, fish, dairy, gluten, sugar, alcohol, or fruit. Basically, these restrictions left me with potatoes and rice since I couldn't digest vegetables, beans, or nuts.

I lost a ton of weight but more importantly, it left me feeling so mentally unwell. I couldn't eat anything; I couldn't go out with friends because I'd have nothing to eat at the restaurant. I was weak, so very weak.

One day, my mom and I were leaving the house to go to, yet again, another doctor. This doctor said everything I was doing was wrong. Ugh, I was so fed up!

The doctor was in Delray Beach and in Delray there's this beautiful street near the

This mindset alone was making me feel sick

water with nice restaurants and boutiques. My mom, seeing my distraught mood leaving the doctor's office, suggested we take a walk and go to a restaurant there.

We sat at a table at what used to be one of my favorite restaurants. I looked at the menu and didn't see one thing I'd be able to eat there. This was more than just eliminating the cheese from a meal, with all the foods I was told I couldn't eat from all the doctors, I would be eliminating basically every ingredient from every meal.

But this didn't feel right. How could this make me healthy when it's just making me weaker and more depressed?

This mindset alone was making me feel sick.

At that moment as the waitress came over to ask for our order, I thought to myself, *you know what, I'm going to listen to each doctor but only take the advice that feels right to me and create my own remedy.*

There it was again, that feeling of relief. A huge weight lifted from my shoulders as soon as I made that decision.

The waitress got my mom's order as I was having this whole conversation in my head and turned to me and asked, "What would you like to order?"

"I'll have the veggie burger, WITH THE FRIES!"

I basically yelled it I was so excited!

Phew, I did it. I ordered actual food. I knew at that moment, I was doing the right thing.

It just felt right. I was so in the present moment after making that decision, I got out of my distraught head, and the heavy weight was lifted.

Once again, the chains wrapped so tightly around my heart, slightly loosened.

After finishing what had to be the best veggie burger and fries I've ever had, I went to use the restroom in the restaurant. No one was in there and as soon as I opened the door, there it was. Just looking at me. Staring up at me from the floor.

Abraham Lincoln.

Another $5 bill facing up.

I looked around, no one came out of this restroom and no one was inside. I bent down, picked it up and that feeling struck me again. That wave of intense emotion, like God was telling me, *Everything is going to be okay. Just trust me.*

I was so in the present moment after making that decision

During this time my mom and I were part of this group called the Dharma Group (*Dharma* means purpose). It was basically a book club of spiritual people who came together for a healthy brunch where everyone brought a dish and we discussed a book we all were reading.

This group was the only place I felt like I could open up and be myself. They understood me because they all have been through their own tragedies.

Every dish someone brought to this brunch was all natural, vegan, and organic. They even asked everyone to write down the ingredients on an index card to put it next to the dish so people knew if they could eat it or not since everyone, not just me for a change, had some type of food issue.

Each conversation I had while part of this Dharma Group was fascinating. People's stories and journeys were all just so incredible. Everyone was so open and vulnerable. It was such a blessing to be part of this group during this tough time of healing.

"Five represents the hand of God"

One brunch, we were sharing stories and I don't know exactly how this came up, but I shared the two experiences I just shared with you: the two times I felt at a crossroads where I stopped resisting my reality and finally surrendered to the moment. And at those two times, a $5 bill presented itself to me.

One of the women in the group was a spiritual leader and after I shared the story she very softly said, "Alexa, do you know what the meaning of five is?"

"No, I don't think so," I responded.

She held up her hand with her palm facing me, as if she were about to wave hello, her fingers widely spread,

"Five represents the hand of God."

The two times when I needed a sign, support, and something to show me the right path, I found a $5 bill.

The moment I eliminated resistance, I found a $5 bill.

The moment I surrendered, I found a $5 bill.

The more we resist, the harder life will be.

The more we try to control what isn't meant to be, the harder life will be.

That doesn't mean you sit back and do nothing. That doesn't mean you give up control over your own life.

It means you stop trying to control the outcome of your actions.

You do the best you can, you give it your all, you listen to your intuition, and *then* you surrender.

You envision the life you want, you dream big, you chase after those dreams, and *then* you surrender.

Stop fighting reality and love what is. When you resist, you suffer. When you surrender, you grow.

Action Step: This week, anytime you feel you are trying to control the situation, wishing it were different, or resisting something, use the mantra *surrender*. Just say it silently to yourself during these moments and as you say it, breathe deeply. Keep this word in your back pocket and use it as a daily mantra.

Another exercise that helps is writing the word *surrender* in your journal 55 times for 5 days in a row. To learn more on why you should write it this many times, Google the "55x5 method".

CHAPTER FIFTEEN

FOMO

I struggle with the fear of missing out.

The fear that there is something better out there than what I'm currently doing in my present moment. The fear of missing out (FOMO) has been extremely present since my college days.

It affects my decision-making skills, my ability to be happy in the present moment, and my confidence in who I am and where I am.

When I lived in my sorority house along with thirty other women my sophomore year of college, I feared missing out on any kind of experience. When I would see a group of girls getting ready for a night out, I felt I had to go out too, even if I didn't really want to; there was no way I wanted to be left out of this experience.

Maybe it wasn't the experience that I was afraid of missing out on but rather feeling *left out*. Growing up, I was part of a big group of friends in middle and high school. While I would be invited to the bigger get togethers or when my parents threw a party and said I could invite my friends, everyone would come (literally one time we had like 500 people show up to a party at my place), I was left out in many other plans. I'd find out my supposedly best friends went to the movies and invited all the girls except me. Or that they were having a sleepover at someone's place and didn't think to call me. There were so many times throughout these years that I felt left out, so maybe that's what triggered these intense feelings of FOMO when I got to college.

There was a period while living in the sorority house that I went out fourteen days in a row in fear of missing out!

I always thought there was something out there that was better than my current reality

This FOMO just got worse as I got older too. I couldn't even figure out what to order anymore when I'd go out to dinner for fear of missing out on a better meal.

I always thought there was something out there that was better than my current reality. Pair that with an insatiable curiosity for life itself and it can get super out of hand. I tried to say yes to everything. I still find myself sometimes doing this because I do want to experience it all and try everything while alive here on this planet, but I also don't want to always be looking outside of my own present life thinking what I have now is not enough.

Because I know it is. That's why struggling with this fear is so challenging for so many. I hear story after story of entrepreneurs struggling with FOMO when it comes to choosing what to focus on in the pursuit towards their dreams.

When you're multi-passionate, that can be extremely challenging (which I personally know all too well). We want to try and do everything under the sun. We want to say yes to all the events in fear of missing out on the connections. We want to say yes to being on every social media platform in fear of missing out on growth opportunities. We want to say yes to every phone call or meeting in fear of missing out on a big deal. We want to say yes to every idea in fear someone else will pursue it before us.

All these fears may lead to complete burnout or worse; they may cause you to lose your passion. You can't be everywhere at once and you most certainly can't be everything to everyone.

So how do you lift this fear of missing out from your life?

Know that where you are right now, literally right now reading this book, is where you are meant to be. You're not supposed to be working on something else. You're not supposed to be reading it someplace else. You're not supposed to be with anyone else. You are, right now, in the here and now at a perfect place for you.

Being confident in the present moment is the first step. But what happens when challenges strike and you need to quickly adapt to the changes? If you are letting the fear of missing out affect your judgement and decisions it will be nearly impossible for you to adapt quickly and successfully. In order to adapt to change and not let this fear impact your ability to decide, you need to know not just which path to say yes to in order to pivot successfully, but how to confidently say no to certain opportunities.

It took me a very long time to overcome this FOMO, and believe me, I still find myself feeling it here and there, but I've finally discovered a few key tricks to help me remove it from my life.

But it took traveling the world to discover this.

During my sophomore year of college, I did what many Jewish college students do, signed up for a free trip to Israel on a Taglit-Birthright trip. Once school ended and summer was upon us, Angela and I boarded a plane along with many of our college friends from the University of Florida and we were off to the Holy Land.

Israel was absolutely breathtaking, the sights, the history, the food, the music, and culture. It was an experience I most definitely will remember forever.

> *It took me a very long time to overcome this FOMO*

When you're on Birthright you have a tour guide from Israel along with your tour guide from the States and program you signed up through. Also, a few Israeli soldiers come along on your trip throughout Israel to, not only act as protection for the group, but to also really learn about the culture and history of Israel.

We happened to be there during Memorial Day and Independence Day, which in the Jewish calendar is different from when we honor those days in America.

Memorial Day, also known as Israel Fallen Soldiers Remembrance Day, takes place the day before Independence Day. It's a national Remembrance Day observed in Israel for all Israeli military personnel who lost their lives in the struggle that led to the establishment of the State of Israel and for those who have been killed subsequently while on active duty in Israel's armed forces.

It was the most beautiful thing I ever experienced

One of the places our tour took us on Memorial Day was a school where we volunteered our time to assist in honoring this significant day. After the ceremony at the school, we all got back on our tour bus to head to our next stop, Tel Aviv.

While sitting there on the bus as we were driving on the highway, I started to hear loud sirens. These sirens were emitting noise throughout the entire country of Israel! Then the most insane thing happened; the bus driver slowed down while on the highway and just stopped, in the middle of the highway! We were directed to get off the bus and when I looked around, every car on the highway was stopped with their driver and passengers standing outside the car on the street. These sirens signaled a moment of silence to honor the fallen soldiers. It was the most beautiful thing I ever experienced, to have an entire country stop, no matter where they were, to take this moment of silence together.

This day definitely brought a lot of emotions and tears, but it followed with so much laughter and joy. What was amazing about the experience was that after you honor the lives lost, you follow it with a celebration for the State of Israel's Independence.

It really shows how all darkness can bring light, if you choose to see it that way.

That night when we got to Tel Aviv, they took us out on the town where all the streets were closed to cars. People were everywhere, drinking, blowing party horns, and waving Israeli flags; it was a huge celebration!

The next morning, on Independence Day, we headed to the beach in Tel Aviv to relax and continue the celebrations. We were all soaking up the sun and recovering from a crazy night out when one of the guys on our trip came back from taking a walk down the beach and said he thought he saw the singer Matisyahu.

Matisyahu is a well-known Israeli singer best known for his song "One Day" that was the anthem for the World Cup back in 2010. Angela and I were big fans so as soon as we heard someone say this, we had to go venture off to see for ourselves if it was really him.

While other people in our group went to go see him from afar, Angela and I took it a step further. He was lying on a beach chair and two other guys were hanging out with him. We worked up the courage to go to the one guy standing up and introduced ourselves, even though we were both just in our bathing suits, making it a bit awkward.

We mentioned we were on Birthright and were big fans of Matisyahu and the friend (who we later learned was his agent) introduced us to him!

...we had to go venture off ...

After hanging out with Matisyahu, a band mate, and his agent for quite some time, they invited us to come back to the recording studio with them after the beach, to record a new song for the album he was working on. Angela and I looked at each other and while we were so tempted to say yes, and almost did say yes, we knew we couldn't.

One, we'd get in so much trouble from ditching our Birthright group (like a ton of trouble) and two, the next stop on our trip was heading to the Bedouin tents in the desert which was a once-in-a-lifetime experience we did not want to miss.

"While we so want to say yes, we have to go see camels in the desert," I said to them following the invitation.

They laughed and tried to convince us why coming with them would be a whole lot more fun. We were struck with two amazing opportunities, and we wish we could've said yes to both, but of course, you can't be in two places at once.

We decided to stick with our group and say yes to the experience in the desert.

Kojak, Matisyahu's agent, got my information and we followed one another on Twitter. I mentioned we'd love to be able to see them when Matisyahu performs in the States. Before we left, we did what we always did at this time, asked Matisyahu for his definition of perfect to add to our "Perfect Is Movement" on *Hello Perfect*.

Matisyahu responded, "Perfect is… there's no such thing is there? How did that word even come into being? Think about it. Is there really such a thing?"

We snapped a photo to remember the moment and said our goodbyes.

Right away we told people in our group about our experience and even our tour guide asked all about it as they were all fans of Matisyahu.

We snapped a photo to remember the moment and said our goodbyes

We then headed on the bus and had a few hours to drive to our next destination, the Bedouin tents. I fell asleep as we were leaving the city of Tel Aviv and when I woke up, I looked out the window and saw camels standing on tall mounds of orange-brown sand! We were just in a major city and now I'm in a desert?! It was the craziest thing to wake up to see camels outside as we were passing by.

When we got off the bus, we stood all around, awaiting our next steps. Our guide pulled out his phone and announced that Matisyahu had just posted on Facebook about two certain girls. What?! Angela and I smiled at each other and everyone in our group looked at us knowing we were the only two who hung out with him.

Our guide began to read his post out loud…

Hung out on Gordon Beach w/@kooolkojak this morning… ran into a group of kids from Florida on a Birthright trip & invited them to come to the studio to check out new music but they were going to ride camels in the desert…

Oh my goodness!

Our guide continued, mentioning that wasn't the best part.

The best part to him, and to everyone in our group, were the comments that were flooding this Facebook post. There were hundreds all trolling us and our guide began to read them out loud to everyone!

Some of the comments included:

Crazy kids, Matisyahu > camels

They did not represent FL very well! Matis/Camels, Matis/Camels…no brainer! OMG, I would have died to go with you! Camels can wait! ♥

Wow once in a lifetime blown. They could ride camels later. Silly kids :)

Hmmmm riding camels in the desert or go to the studio with Matisyahu and chill listening to sick beats? No brainer there!

i wish i would have been one of those kids, i would have made the right choice

*Ride camels over hangin with you? *shaking my head**

Everyone began to laugh, and while yes, we did miss out on this, probably once-in-a-lifetime opportunity, we had to make a

We had a super early wake up call

decision, as we couldn't have both experiences. Sure, we imagined what it would've been like to hang in the studio with him, and I'm sure it probably would have been amazing, but that night and next morning, proved to be one of the best experiences I've had traveling.

We spent the night in the desert at the Bedouin tents, eating authentic Israeli food on the floor, learning about their history, and yes, hanging with the camels. Angela and I ventured off from the group to do our own exploring (probably not allowed but so worth it) and enjoyed some Hookah with our Israeli friends.

We had a super early wake up call to climb the famous ancient fortress Masada before the sun rose. We all did not want to do this as we were exhausted from the previous nights and days of partying, but we followed our guide and we got to the top of Masada just as the sun was rising. Our Israeli tour guide brought a stereo with him and as we sat there and watched the sun slowly rise above the desert hills, he played "Here Comes the Sun" by The Beatles. Now this was a moment I would never forget.

I went to sleep that next night without one ounce of regret for the decision made.

It was this experience in Israel on Birthright that helped me overcome some of my FOMO struggles. If I let my fear of missing out win, I would have spent time with Matisyahu, true; however, I would've never experienced that magical moment climbing to the top of Masada. If I let my FOMO affect my ability to be in the present moment, I wouldn't have been able to enjoy all that I did get to experience, always wondering if I made the wrong choice or fearing I missed out on something better.

I never once questioned this while there and what I realized is yes, we will most definitely miss out on some cool experiences in our life because we can't possibly be in two places at once, but that does not mean what you're doing now is not just as good or better.

There is magic in the present moment and magic in believing you are exactly where you are supposed to be. When you can live in the present moment and be confident in where you are, that's when you'll begin to experience so many other wonders of the world around you.

And I truly believe that when you are following the flow of life and listening to your intuition, you'll have the opportunity for many exciting, once-in-a-lifetime experiences.

Fast forward to seven months after our Birthright trip, we saw that Matisyahu was scheduled for a concert in South Florida. I decided to take my shot and see if they remembered us. I tweeted Kojak a private message and asked if we'd be able to meet up with Matisyahu while he was in town, reminding him we were the girls from Florida that chose camels over studio time with them.

We ended up scoring backstage passes for that concert thanks to Kojak and once again, got to hang out a bit with Matisyahu and have another memorable experience with my best friend.

In life, everything comes with sacrifices. If you want to start your own business, you may have to sacrifice weekends out with friends. If you want to start a family and save for retirement, you may have to sacrifice some vacation experiences. If you want to finish writing your book, you may have to sacrifice time spent on social media.

The key I discovered on how to overcome the fear of missing out is to understand how to evaluate the opportunity cost for each experience presented to you.

When you know how to put a value on each item, you can make more confident decisions, adapt quickly to change, and be certain

There is magic in the present moment

in the direction your life is headed, regardless of how many times you have to pivot or say no to certain experiences.

I had to really get that fear of missing out eliminated from my mindset if I wanted to plan my wedding, finish my manuscript, and launch a whole new division of my company in one year. I had to be okay with missing out on going to conferences I knew all my industry friends would be at and I had to be okay with seeing my friends on social media going out and having fun experiences while I was at home writing.

But the opportunity cost of *not* writing my book far outweighed the cost of missing these experiences.

So today, every time I am hit with a decision, I strategically take time to value the opportunity cost of each, but then once I make a decision, I remain confident in it. I allow myself to be present and enjoy every moment of *my life*, not wondering or wishing I was someplace else.

FOMO brings nothing positive to your life. It doesn't allow you to experience it all. It doesn't help you not miss out on things. All it leads to are feelings of self-doubt, low confidence, and living in a comparison mindset.

I've come a long way since my college days, but as I mentioned, the FOMO still does hit me every now and then. I mean, I'm only human. When this happens, I notice the fear and then I take a step back and weigh the two, three, or sometimes even five different options and work to make a decision. From that point on I let all other things go and I remain focused on that decision.

Remember, in order to be able to adapt to any change thrown your way you must be able to not only know which way to pivot but know how to say no to opportunities. That is the key to always being the one in charge of your own life and on course towards achieving your biggest dreams, regardless of the challenges that come your way.

Right now, you are in the exact place you are meant to be. Everything up to this point has helped you become the person you are meant to become.

Trust the journey, trust your decisions, and trust yourself. Every experience has the opportunity to bring magic into your life, if you are present enough to witness and appreciate it.

Action Step: List out some experiences you are feeling FOMO around. Are you in fear you're missing out on a fun trip with friends if you decide to stay home with your family? Are you in fear you'll miss out on growing your brand if you decide to take a break from social media for a week? Are you in fear of missing out on hanging with industry friends at a big conference if you decide to stay home and save the money?

After writing out your list, put a numerical value on the opportunity cost of each experience with one being the potential gain, low, and ten, high.

For Example:

Going to an industry conference because friends are going or saving the money for our wedding and honeymoon.

Industry Event: Opportunity Cost = 5

Wedding & Honeymoon: Opportunity Cost = 10

Now to help me get to those values, I did think about the event and what could be my return on investment. Would that event potentially help me grow my business and income? Did I have to go to be able to hear someone speak or meet someone there? Or is the decision being impacted by feelings of the fear of missing out because I know a bunch of people going and want to be included in the fun? I realized it was the latter. FOMO was impacting this decision and these feelings of uncertainty about what to do. If it were the former where I believed it was necessary to go for my dreams and business, I would go because the opportunity cost would be way hgher and then I would have to fi gure out somethng else to sacrifi ce to then be able to stll save the money for our wedding and honeymoon.

This is exactly what you want to decipher from this exercise: whether you are making a smart decision based on your goals or a decision driven by the fear of missing out. The latter will always leave you feeling burnt out and not in control of your own life and direction. When you follow the fear, you'll end up missing out on something that is more important to you because every single opportunity you say yes to, means you are saying no to something else.

Another example:

Enjoying my Sundays relaxing or exploring pop-up festivals and events: Opportunity Cost = 2

Finish writing my book: Opportunity Cost = 10

When I see people on social media doing all these fun things on the weekends, that fear of missing out is most certainly present. It causes me to feel like I'm doing life wrong or that I'm not living my life to the fullest, which is such a horrible feeling to have. But when I complete this exercise, I realize the opportunity cost of *not* staying home and writing my book far outweighs a few fun Sundays.

The key here is to use this exercise to help you make the right decision for you and your future. You want to make decisions that will help you get closer to living the life of your dreams and living life on your own terms doing what *you* really want to do and not what the fear is telling you that you should do.

CHAPTER SIXTEEN

The Blame Game

The more we blame, the less ownership we have over our future and life.

We want to live a life we love, filled with joy, health, laughter, success, and love, yet when things go wrong, we are the last person to take ownership over those things.

We blame others.
We blame the circumstances.
We blame life.

Yes, there are things out of our control.

There are things I wish I could change… about society, about the past, about my chronic illness…

But what would it do for me to merely complain without any action?

Will complaining change the past? No.
Will complaining make my condition go away? No.
Will complaining do anything productive? No.

What I can do is be open to learning from others. What I can do is speak up. What I can do is spread awareness.

You must always believe, regardless of the circumstances, that you have complete ownership over your future. Not because you can or should try to control the outcome, as previously mentioned, but because you have the power to control the actions you take and the way you choose to show up in the world every single day.

It's not a fact. It's a *mindset*.

This mindset is critical because if at one moment you believe you don't have ownership over your future, you are more likely to give up. More likely to forfeit. More likely to stay in a victim mindset.

I was in a victim mindset for years in my twenties and it was no fun at all.

We can complain or we can act.

We can take control over our own life, or we can put it in the hands of someone else.

◆◆◆

I've blamed my near-death experience for the onset of my autoimmune disease.
I've blamed my autoimmune disease for the reason I lost so many dreams.
I've blamed my family for stress that made me severely ill.
I've blamed my friends for my feeling lonely.

I've done it all because I'm human just like you and unfortunately, it's natural to blame everyone else before we take back control of our life and our happiness.

> *Stop blaming yourself for the past. Stop blaming yourself for things that went wrong*

You don't need to go blaming others and you most definitely don't need to go blaming yourself.

That's the last thing I'd want for you because blame only makes people feel bad. It makes other people feel bad when they feel they caused something negative for you and it makes you feel bad about yourself if you take the blame over wrong things in your life.

I'm not the reason I have an autoimmune disease. I didn't do that to myself so there is no need to feel bad about myself for that or blame myself for it. Same for your current or past circumstances.

Stop blaming yourself for the past. Stop blaming yourself for things that went wrong. Just get blame out of your life; it doesn't serve anyone, and it most definitely doesn't bring about any positivity.

But understand this: Blame and ownership are two very different things.

Ownership over your life means you and you alone, have the power to change your life at any moment for the better.

It means you are no longer the victim but the victor.

You can create any future you dream. You can achieve anything you want.

This mindset is to empower you. Yes, there are things out of our control, but again, you must always believe that there is opportunity ahead for you, something greater for you, if you continue to move forward.

The happier I am, the healthier I become

Complaining, blaming—none of that will help you achieve anything. It will only make you feel worse about yourself and your life.

I used to complain that I had to go sit in an infusion center every eight weeks for three hours next to people that were four times my age, but that mindset led me to feel sicker.

I promise that through everything I've learned along my health journey, I have found that there is a direct correlation between my health and happiness.

The happier I am, the healthier I become.

So, if I want to be healthy, I must do everything in my power to protect my perception of my current circumstances. If every eight weeks when I go get my infusion I complain and feel like a victim to my illness, it will only make me feel sad about my life and therefore, sicker.

While at first, I viewed this as a limitation, having to rely on medicine to keep me healthy, needing the best health insurance to be able to afford this medicine, and always having to work my travel schedule around this infusion schedule. One day, after being tired of feeling like a victim of circumstance, I decided to shift my perception. (That's always the first step, to make the firm decision.)

I started to say before I left the house, "I'm going to get my superpowers!"

This medicine heals me, so isn't that a superpower?!

Yep, I'd say so! And isn't it something to be grateful about, medical innovation that saved my entire life? Of course!

We all have some type of limitation in our life. Whether it is something to do with your health, body, mind, financial situation, current location, support system, or any number of things, we all have limits.

You can choose to continue to look at them with the perspective that they are limiting you from achieving your full potential or you can view them as what makes you stand out, helps you gain incomparable strength, and teaches you invaluable lessons.

It all comes down to perspective.

Your limitation just may be your superpower, if you choose to see it that way.

Since I turned my complaining into gratitude, I actually look forward to going to get my infusion. I see it as a three-hour window where I can just relax, read a book, or listen to a podcast while my superpowers are running through my veins.

You can do this with many things in your life, through a simple change in thought.

What you choose to focus on is your choice.

You can always find something to complain about, but you can also always find something to be grateful for.

Action Step: Be mindful of playing the blame game. Next time something goes wrong, notice how you react. Are you blaming your partner, your mom or dad, a friend, or even yourself? When this happens, stop your thoughts in the act, take a deep breath, and journal the experience.

Write out how you feel, why you feel that way, whom you are blaming, and then let yourself be free from it. Either write out how you are letting it go or a solution to the problem.

Don't focus on the cause, keep your focus on the release or the solution. Remember, your energy is precious and by focusing on blaming someone or something for a current problem in your life, you are redirecting your energy from focusing on things that will help move your life in the direction you want. The direction you deserve.

CHAPTER SEVENTEEN

Don't Let This Live Inside of You

Resentment is a horrible thing to carry around.

It's like a dark cloud you choose to carry with you. It'll always be there just lingering above you or inside of you.

You don't realize how it affects you unless you are in the environment or near the person you resent but any negative feeling like resentment does have an impact on the overall energy you give out in this world.

It takes some of your light, leaving you less able to shine.

And we do not want that ever to happen!

◆◆◆

I've held on to resentment for years. I've resented my dad, my mom, my best friend, my sister, my external family, people I didn't even know…

And it was such a horrible feeling I carried around.

While I thought the resentment was something I needed to have to show them their actions hurt me, this was farthest from the truth. The resentment was just hurting me.

I was in pain having these feelings towards people I loved dearly. Why was I holding on to such a horrible feeling?

Well at first, I didn't realize I was doing it intentionally. But every time I saw that person I resented, a horrible negative feeling would come up to the point where I felt a big ball in the middle of my chest causing me pain.

This almost caused me to be in a state of hatred instead of love.

Nothing, and I mean *nothing* in this world—no person, no experience, no material thing, no job—is ever worth stealing away your light.

I didn't notice I was holding on to so much resentment until it started to cause my mom and me to have ongoing fights, which we never used to have.

She is my best friend and we'd always gotten along so well until the year my mom and dad moved to Dallas, TX for a job opportunity and I decided to stay in South Florida. Now that I was finally able to be on my own, without my mom taking care of me, I wanted to begin this new chapter in my life with a focus on my happiness and mental well-being. Although I was ready to leave this darkness in the past, my mom was still going through her own personal and marital struggles. We were in two different places, both physically and emotionally. It was difficult, because she has always been right by my side as my mom, best friend, and biggest cheerleader, and so I had this inherent expectation of her to still be that positive person lifting me up, yet this time, it was her sadness that I felt was affecting my ability to find the happiness I was searching for.

I was always there for my mom during these hard times, and she was always there for me, but when the hard emotions she was dealing with unintentionally began taking a toll on me, I started to recognize a sense of resentment building and I held onto it for a very long year.

It was a very selfish feeling to have, but after being in complete darkness and sadness for five years at this time, I was ready to let it all go and I'd do anything to not bring it back… including separating myself from the people I loved more than I wanted to.

I found myself resenting my dad for moving my mom to Texas and then leaving her by herself when he lived and worked in China for months on end. I resented my mom for still being sad when I just wanted to be happy and to make her happy. I resented my friends for leaving me during these challenging years. I resented myself for even having these feelings towards the people I love.

It wasn't until my family decided to move to Raleigh, North Carolina so we could all be close to one another, that things began to change.

Shortly after making the transition to Raleigh, I remember crying and sitting on my bed in my parents' house, feeling like I didn't belong there and wondering what happened to my life I loved, once again feeling like it was just ripped up from under me.

Somehow it came up how I felt towards her and she said to me, very kindly and softly,

"Why are you holding on to resentment and keeping it inside of you?"

You know when you've heard a lesson over and over again but then someone says it in a different way and it just clicks?

This was that moment.

How she said it just clicked and I remember thinking at that moment, *"Resentment is something I'm choosing to hold on to and it's causing me pain. But if I am the one choosing to hold on to it, that means I can also choose to let it go."*

It had been within my power all along.

I didn't need time to heal things.

I didn't need an apology.

I didn't need someone to do it for me and fix everything...

The only person I needed was myself and a decision to LET IT GO.

Is it easy to let it go? Heck no!

Is it worth it? Most definitely.

One of my favorite sayings is, "forgiveness is for you," and I think the same thing goes when speaking to letting things go. Letting go of what happened in the past does not mean you don't hold a person who hurt you accountable for their actions. It does not mean the pain is not real and is not still there.

It is simply a decision to help you feel peace along the path of healing. Does it happen overnight after you make the decision? No way! It takes time to heal and everyone has their own journey, but just know your peace and space in your mind and heart is worth way more than the actions others have done to cause you pain.

Do it for you.

Let whatever is preventing you from being happy go.

We can't change the past, but we can change our actions and thoughts towards healing from the past.

Trust things happened for a reason.

Understand that holding on to resentment is keeping you from truly enjoying all the good that life will bring you.

If it isn't serving you, let it go.

If you can't do anything about it, let it go.

If it's causing you pain, let it go.

If you want to live a life filled with joy, let it go.

Action Step: Think of anything or anyone you've felt resentment towards. To help you let it go, write a letter to them. Don't worry, you aren't going to give them the letter, this is just for you. Write how you feel and explain why you have this resentment towards them. Then re-read it out loud to yourself. While you are doing that, visualize the resentment as a dark cloud inside of you getting pulled out with every word you say until the end of the letter when the dark cloud is removed and fully released from within you. Now tear up the letter and say, *"I'm letting this go!"*

CHAPTER EIGHTEEN

One Word in One Sentence

Every person reading this book is interpreting it differently. You are reading the exact same words yet how you perceive it will be different. One chapter may resonate strongly with you but not someone else, simply because of past circumstances or current feelings.

This is because our perception creates our reality. And you always have the power to see your life through a different lens.

The key to becoming adaptable is to **see things not as they are, but rather as they *can* be.**

For years I dreaded waking up in the morning. Not because I had to go to school, work, or that I'm not a morning person (because I most definitely am) but because the mornings were the worst when it came to the pain my autoimmune disease would bring on.

For a good three years as I was struggling with constant flare ups and no sign of relief, I would start my days in the bathroom for hours on end. Many times, I'd find myself curled up in the fetal position on my bathroom floor crying in pain. It was unbearable and it's how I started my day, every day, for three solid years.

The pain would leave me feeling so weak; it was truly an effort to try and accomplish anything else that day. Once I did find the strength to finally stand up, I'd look into my mirror, at my sunken in, pale face and question:

"Why did this happen to me?
Why did this have to happen to me?
I'm only 23 years old, I don't know how I'm going to be able to live the rest of my life like this."

Day after day this was my conversation with myself in my bathroom mirror, until one day I was so fed up. I was fed up with being the victim of ulcerative colitis.

I was fed up with waiting until I'd get my old life back, realizing after six months turned into years of this reality, that I'd *never* get my old life back. I'm different now. I have to live with this chronic illness for the rest of my life.

And if I must live with this, I have to accept it and not fight it.

I have to embrace that having this illness is very much part of me, but it does not define me. It does not define what I can or cannot do.

I was waiting for something to change until I felt I could live my life again. But what I was really doing was trying to bring back the past; trying to take away this reality that felt so strange to me, so foreign. This wasn't my life. I was supposed to be still living in New York City with my best friend and taking over the world with my blog.

I wasn't supposed to be living back with my mom and having her as my caretaker. This wasn't my life and I did not want to accept it.

But every morning there was no way to avoid the pain. I had a constant reminder every waking moment that this was my reality, this was my *new normal.*

One day, as I worked up the strength to stand back up again after a horrible morning of feeling ill, I looked again at my sunken, bony, pale face in my bathroom mirror. I looked into my eyes and saw, for the first time: past the pain, past the hollowness, past the victim.

And this morning, instead of asking myself "*Why did this happen to me?*" I asked myself,

"Why did this happen *for* me?"

This change in *one* word in this *one* sentence brought about a huge change. Not because I felt better or that I suddenly was cured from this autoimmune disease, but because I shifted my perception of it.

I stopped falling victim to my circumstances.

Instead of seeing my illness as an obstacle I'd never overcome, I chose to perceive my new reality as an opportunity. An opportunity for something bigger than myself. I didn't know what it was yet, but I just knew at that moment, all of this happened for a reason.

I chose to see my life not as it was, but rather as it could be.

When you feel like life is against you, when everything is going wrong, when you question how you will continue to go on, remember, all you have to do is shift the perspective of your current reality.

You must believe that things happen FOR you versus TO you. Every challenge, every obstacle, every tragedy along this journey has helped you find the person you are meant to become.

Don't wait until you feel you have it all together or your life is "perfect." You don't need to have it all together to inspire others.

Heck, I'm still going through so many challenges and here I am trying to inspire you.

We tend to think we will change the way we feel once our circumstances change, but our circumstances change once we change the way we feel.

You always have the power to change your life in an instant with a thought.

Positive change stems from one thought, one emotion, one feeling. This is where it starts. You must work to BE the person you want to become, today. That is the only way to change your current circumstances.

Action Step: Choose one thing in your life that is *affecting* you. It can be a relationship, something going on in your business, uncertainty about the future, or financial challenges. Pick something very specific. Then in your journal, fill in the below.

How it is:

How it can be:

Describe your current situation, how you currently are perceiving it. Then, imagine how it can be if you shifted every part of that paragraph you just wrote.

For example:

How it is: I have a chronic autoimmune disease that I must live with for the rest of my life. I'll never feel 100% healthy again. I have to live day in and day out in pain for nothing. Why did I have to get this autoimmune disease from my near-death experience, why couldn't it all just be in my past? This is going to prevent me from accomplishing everything I want.

How it can be: I have an inspiring story to share. My autoimmune disease has been hard but because of that, I now have become extremely empathetic and can relate to others on a much deeper level. This experience will help me become a world-class speaker and one day possibly a best-selling author. While it sucks, it'll be worth it because it will help change thousands of others' lives showing that even when you are struggling, you can still chase after your dreams.

CHAPTER NINETEEN

Exchange Hope for Curiosity

"Just have hope."

This was the advice I'd constantly hear. To have hope. But what happens when you can't find the hope? What happens when you are in so much pain, you're suffering from tragedy, and you don't want to go on... where is *hope*?

I hated this advice. I hated it because as someone who has a chronic, incurable disease, there is no hope for a cure. So, this, to me, felt like empty advice.

It just led me to feeling worse about my current life and the future ahead.

But after that morning in the bathroom when I started to ask myself, "Why did this happen *for* me?" a new chord struck.

◆◆◆

Questioning why this happened FOR me, FOR a reason, led me to being curious to discover what that reason may be.

I became so curious that I found myself passionate about sharing my story as a public speaker. I thought, if this happened for a reason, then maybe my story can inspire someone else on their journey.

I pitched myself to sixty different local organizations to speak at their monthly meetup, for free, and received sixty rejections or no responses. After months of doing this, I felt so discouraged.

I was waiting until one of these event organizers gave me permission to speak and I thought, "Well if no one is giving me the opportunity to speak, I guess I can't be a public speaker!"

Until that fire of passion became so strong... so strong that I felt I *had* to get up in front of others and share my story *now* or else I wouldn't be able to continue on. I couldn't wait any longer until someone decided to believe in me.

That's when I realized by waiting for permission, I was putting my dream in the hands of these strangers.

Don't ever put your dreams in the hands of a stranger!

I was relying on hope to become a speaker, hoping that someone would hire me and give me a chance.

But hope is not a strategy!

That's when I took my dreams back into my own hands.

When no one would give me an opportunity to speak, I started my own local meetup group and hosted my first event which had five people in attendance. I was ecstatic! Each event I hosted after that grew.

And even when things didn't work out or go as planned, that insatiable curiosity drove me.

I became so curious to what may happen if I sent one more email, made one more phone call, or hosted one more event.

Through this journey of curiosity, as I like to call it, I found *myself* again.

I had a sense of motivation and purpose every morning. So even when I didn't feel well or had to suff er through the pain, it was all worth it. That curiosity led me to one of the greatest adventures of my life, the pursuit toward my purpose.

I didn't look at the future and think, there's no hope for me. Instead, I looked at the future with a curious soul and questioned, *What's out there for me?*

Having curiosity leads you to taking one step a day. No matter how many times you feel you are moving backwards, you'll move forward step by step, persevering—questioning what may happen if you don't give up.

When you are curious, you find a way to make it happen.

You become adaptable to any change because you want to discover what lies ahead for you and you will do anything to figure it out.

During tough times, I offer this advice: **Exchange hope for curiosity.**

Become extremely curious about what may happen if you don't give up. If you make one more phone call, if you pivot one more time, if you send one more pitch, if you attend one more networking event, if you make one more post on social media, if you say hello to one more person…

It only takes one thing to change your entire life for the better, but you must have the curiosity to discover it.

And one thing I can promise to you, is that...

Curiosity, when paired with perseverance, will eventually, and always, lead you to re-discovering hope.

Action Step: What are you curious about when it comes to your dreams and goals? Are you curious about how it will feel, who you will meet along the way, what the money will do for you, what the adventure has in store for you…?

Write out three action steps you are taking right now that you've been working on for some time to achieve a goal and pair those steps with a curious thought.

Example:

Action step: Reaching out to sponsors for my event.
Curiosity: What if this next sponsor (the 50th one I've called) says yes…

Action step: Pitching my book proposal to agents.
Curiosity: What if this next agent says yes…

Action step: Posting videos on YouTube.
Curiosity: What if this next video goes viral…

HOPE.

Your life can change in an instant. Even when you think you've hit rock bottom, it can get worse, but it can also get better. So how do you prevail in darkness when you can't see any light?

Hope. You call on hope. She lives within every single one of us yet many of us don't take time to talk to her. We don't believe she is there and soon we question if she even exists. I've asked myself many times, "What is hope?" and now I've finally begun to realize what hope is.

Hope is a word that is almost as abstruse as love.

A four-letter singular word that has the power to make us feel like we can keep going, hope keeps us from giving up. It is like a person in the back of a broken-down car who keeps on pushing the car uphill. When we lose hope though, it can shatter us into a million little pieces.

Hope is something extraordinary. It is not something you can hold in your hand, but it is something you can give to others.

It is nearly impossible to describe hope because it is unique to each one of us. We can find hope in laughter, in prayer, or in friendship. Or we can be blinded by the hope that surrounds us and feel at a loss.

So, what really is hope and when will it find us?

I will be the first to admit that there have been times when I feel hopeless.

Close your eyes for a moment.

What do you see?

Darkness.

That is what it feels like when there is no hope.

You see, hope is the light in your darkness. It is the pusher, the motivator, and the very thing that brings us into an existence of love.

I first found hope when I was lying in the intensive care unit in a coma. I saw it. The light, the colors, and the understanding that there is more of my life to be lived.

That hope helped me wake up from that coma. It helped me heal myself when I only had a 1% chance left. It proved the doctors wrong when they told my mom I only had 24 hours to live.

That is hope. The feeling that you can survive. The knowing that this pain, this struggle, this tragedy is only temporary.

You see hope is not temporary. Hope is infinite.

There will always be hope for you to find. Sometimes when we need it the most, we ask why it hasn't shown up for us. We feel like this is the end, that there is nothing left for the world to offer us, and that this pain and misery will always be our reality.

But you see, hope doesn't search for you, you have to find it.

It lives within you. Deep inside. In your soul.

Sometimes, hope can be passed along from soul to soul. Hope gives us the power to save others and help them see the light again in their darkness.

So maybe hope is our actions. Maybe hope is the way we think. Or maybe, it has nothing to do with anything. Maybe hope is just there, like a little glass bottle we can drink whenever we need its special powers.

All I know for sure is that pain may be real, but so is hope, if only you are curious enough to re-discover it.

CHAPTER TWENTY

Empathy

Many friends and family will disappear when you're going through tough times... especially challenges that last for a prolonged period of time.

Friends won't understand you.

They'll say to be grateful for what you have.

They'll say to get over it already.

Don't take it in. Understand that *they don't understand*. It is not until others go through hard times that they can truly relate.

When they experience something personally, whether it's a chronic illness, depression, mental health issues... that's when they will finally be able to see you. And *truly* see you. That's when they'll understand how to be the friend you need.

After my near-death experience, I was suffering for years figuring out how to live with my autoimmune disease. And through those years, I lost family, close friends, and I lost connection to a lot of people I truly cared about.

While people may be able to handle a few months of your sadness, very few people will be able to stick by your side when those months turn into years.

There was a time along my health journey (almost a year) when I was too sick to leave my apartment, to the point where I could barely walk my dog outside.

Even after vulnerably sharing with my friends and some external family members how I was feeling, asking them to come over once in a while to just watch a movie or sit with me, no one did.

They would say, "Yeah of course," but these were just empty words as a year went by and not one person ever came over.

People tend to stray when the times are too challenging and either they don't want to deal with your problems, or they don't know how to be there for you, so they eventually disappear.

It's the same thing when it comes to death: people will purposely not call or text someone thinking that's the better answer because they don't know *what* to say and they justify it by saying that person probably wants their space.

No!

That person wants and needs to feel supported.

That year where I felt stuck in my apartment because I was too sick to leave, where it was just my mom and me, it would have meant the world to me if a friend just texted me: Thinking about you. <3

That's all. How long does it take to text that? How much effort is that to show someone who you supposedly care about and who is in pain, that they are on your mind?

Day after day, nobody texted.

Day after day I felt more lonely, more forgotten.

I used to hold so much resentment towards those people too. Thinking they weren't there for me, didn't care, and just let me go during my toughest times only to return when I'm happy.

This resentment built up over the years and I let a lot of those people go. I felt so angry at them. I felt like they just threw me to the curbside when I needed them.

But one thing I learned through healing, is that this wasn't their fault.

> *I learned how resentment was a terrible thing to have inside of me, so I let it go*

Their actions of not being there for me when I needed them wasn't their fault. They just couldn't understand. Everyone perceives life from their own point of view and that's dependent on circumstances and environment.

They didn't know *how* to be there for me. They couldn't relate.

But that didn't make them bad people. That didn't mean they necessarily didn't care about me.

Later on in my journey as I found health again, I reconnected with a few of those friends and at first, the resentment built up when I saw them. I could feel that big lump of anger in my chest, of abandonment, of feeling they were fake.

As I mentioned earlier, I learned how resentment was a terrible thing to have inside of me, so I let it go.

It was affecting me more than it was affecting anyone else, and I didn't want to be this person who walked around with resentment. Such a horrible thing to have living inside of you.

I turned that resentment into gratitude. I began to separate myself from others, not trying to make them understand me but instead, I felt gratitude that my experiences and all my challenges, taught me how to have empathy.

Empathy, to me, is like a unique superpower in this world. Many will say they have it, but they'll confuse it with sympathy or compassion.

Empathy is having the ability to literally put yourself in someone else's shoes; to actually *feel* someone else's feelings.

It's not a matter of hearing how this person is struggling and then trying to "fix them" by offering advice (ugh I hated when people would try and tell me what foods to eat and what doctors to see to heal). I get that they were trying to help but it was really frustrating when others who didn't know my full journey tried to fix me.

People who are going through tough times just need someone to listen to them. I'm not talking about the kind of listening where it goes in through one ear and out the other. I mean truly hearing them by providing the feeling of comfort, support, and letting the person know they aren't alone.

I believe that it will be the empathetic leaders who truly change the world. It will be the leaders who have gone through so many challenges and struggles yet instead of feeling resentment towards their past or others, they find gratitude in how they grew. Gratitude for the empathetic person they became.

If people are important to you, they'll find their way back into your life. And if they mean something to you, you'll let them back in. You'll learn how to accept them for who they are, accept them for how they deal with challenges, knowing that everyone's journey is different and everyone handles things differently. And once you let them back in, you'll likely find that they apologize for not having been there for you. They will tell you that they simply didn't know how to support you.

Remember, forgiveness is for **you.**

This will allow you to live a very full life, surrounded by good people. It will allow you to be there for others in your own way, not expecting anything in return from them.

You will no longer be a victim of others' actions.

You'll know that not everyone will understand what you're going through, and that's okay. It mightalso aff ord you that glance from the others' perspective, and it might give you the strength to say to a friend in need, "I don't know how to support you, but if you'll tell me, I can try."

Action Step: Practice empathy today by calling a friend or family member and just listening to what they have to say and being present in the conversation. Don't off er advice or don't bring the conversation back to yourself with an experience you had. Just listen and tell them you are there for them. Use your heart to connect so they can truly feel you are there and that you understand to the best of your ability.

CHAPTER TWENTY-ONE

Community

My community saved my life.

It's the most important thing to me when it comes to my career- *you*.

The people I serve.

You are the reason I wake up every day feeling motivated to keep going.

If you don't have a community to turn to in your professional and personal life, you are missing out on one of the greatest experiences as a human.

Connection is powerful, but it must be real—not surface-level.

The moment you decide to be courageous enough to share not just your successes, but the failures, the hardships, the struggles you are currently going through with others, while you are still chasing after your dreams, is the moment you'll be able to find your true community.

When you share your challenges, you give others permission to share theirs as well.

If we continue to hide them inside of ourselves, we are blocking part of our heart, therefore not being fully open to discover our full potential.

Think of your heart as a Mason jar. Every challenge or obstacle you've experienced in your life is represented by a pebble.

Whether that challenge was in middle school when someone bullied you, in college when you didn't get elected for that leadership position you wanted, or later in your life when you and your partner experienced a miscarriage, those challenges shaped you. From challenges that came and went to ones that were much bigger, each one is a pebble.

And every time you go through one, a pebble gets dropped into the Mason jar.

Now, every time you decide to embrace that experience by sharing it with others and not allowing it to weigh you down by hiding it away from the world, that pebble gets tossed out of the jar. It's still part of you because it left its mark, but it's no longer taking up space inside of your heart.

The more pebbles you have inside the jar, the less room there is for everything else, like love, connection, success, exciting memories, and more.

When you surround yourself with a community who truly supports you and accepts you for who you are, that's when you are able to gain the courage to toss the pebbles out of your Mason jar, one by one.

When I was going through a tough time with my autoimmune disease, during that long year of being stuck inside my apartment, I had started to go live every morning on a new live streaming app. I created a morning show called, *Morning Motivation with Alexa* where I would go live Monday through Friday at 10:00 a.m. eastern and speak on a certain topic motivating my audience.

But when I started to get sicker and sicker, I knew I couldn't authentically get on live and be positive and motivating when I was struggling so much inside.

I was faced with a choice: stop the show until I felt better or share vulnerably what I was going through.

I knew there was no end in sight for this health journey and so I decided to share vulnerably; I decided to share everything I was going through. The days I didn't feel motivated, I'd share the experience with them. I would live stream from my bed on some days because I was too weak to get out of it.

I went from twenty to fifty people tuning in live to hundreds, sometimes even thousands, tuning in live in a matter of weeks, simply by being real.

What I realized is people could relate more to me just being open and honest with them and that itself was the inspiring message they needed to see and hear.

This vulnerability and transparency led me to form close connections with my community. So close, in fact, that many flew to my Women Empower X events to meet me. Those who found me at my most vulnerable, still follow me today, and have become my greatest brand advocates.

Every morning when I felt like I should just give up, it was my community waiting for me to go live that motivated me to stay resilient.

I truly believe they helped save my life.

This sense of community, the importance of it, has been a foundation for everything I've done since. WEX is rooted in community, heck we even grew that way: completely in a grass-roots way from word of mouth.

The more people you know the faster you will grow.

·· Adaptable

That's why we also created the WEX membership community: to be able to provide that authentic connection for people around the world. A community who truly supports and embraces one another, a community that is truly diverse and inclusive, a community that cheers one another on, rooted in collaboration over competition.

There is no reason people should be competing against one another on their journey towards their dreams. If I learned anything from my community, it's that **there is enough room for all of us to be successful!** Find your community by being open, vulnerable, and transparent with them.

Make sure you invest time into growing your relationships.

This connection, this support, will enable you to achieve far more than you could alone. Not because you aren't capable but because when you feel supported, you feel more empowered than ever to take that bigger risk, knowing if you don't succeed you still have us to fall back on and lift you up to keep going.

Community fuels empowerment and when you feel that, it's almost like a superpower; you feel like you can do anything.

Invest in finding an online community to help you grow your dreams.

Everyday share who you are with them: what you are going through, your wins, and your losses.

This is one of my company's core values. It's amazing what can happen when you have a few good people by your side. Just imagine thousands of people cheering you on and lifting you up as you work to achieve what you once could only imagine.

How would that feel?

Find your community. And love them hard.

Action Step: Create an ongoing calendar reminder once a week to remind yourself to reach out to at least one person. Whether it is a friend, a colleague, or a broad community on social media. The more people you know, the faster you will grow but for that to be true, you need to not just know them, you need to stay *connected* to them, in an *authentic* way.

Start today by writing down five people's names in your journal you want to reach out to this week. These could be people you know, want to get to know, or even someone you follow online. You never know what may happen as I believe it only takes one person to potentially transform your life forever.

CHAPTER TWENTY-TWO

Become Non-Hackable

When it comes to our computers and tech devices, we do everything under the sun to make sure they are non-hackable. We download software, we buy the best systems, we ensure we create unique passwords, all to protect others from getting inside.

Now why don't we do this for our own body and mind?

The supercomputer inside you needs to be protected.

If you don't pay attention to this, all of a sudden, you'll live your entire life realizing you were controlled by everyone else.

Controlled by your parents' wishes.

Controlled by society setting the timeline of your life.

Controlled by friends deciding your choices.

It is so easy to be influenced and "hacked" by others and that is why it is imperative to protect your own supercomputer… your mind, body, and soul.

Most people won't ever realize the scars others are leaving behind inside of them because those scars are invisible. Many times, you won't even realize others are influencing your decisions because ultimately, you are the last decision maker, making the choices for yourself.

But we have to pay attention to this or else you will forever live someone else's life or worse, you will live a life full of struggle, regret, and hardship.

♦♦♦

I experienced it firsthand, in a way that was most definitely not invisible.

After a year of using food and holistic remedies to heal my body and get into remission with my autoimmune disease, I was finally feeling healthy again. I was no longer this frail, weak individual but instead, I was stronger, happier, and just looked more alive.

And while I was on the mend, outside circumstances tested me once again.

My dad was not in a good place. His business was failing, his marriage was splitting, and all this was stressing him so badly that he fell back into troubling habits.

My parents had a lot of challenges to work through, causing fights to be a constant in my household.

My mom wasn't feeling well and she ended up getting a colonoscopy. The doctor found something, and I still remember the day the doctor said that horrible "c" word to us.

I went into defensive mode. It can't be. There's no way.

I started to pray every second I got. I needed to be strong for my mom because I'm the only one she had nearby to lean on. But I needed someone to lean on as well. I felt so alone.

My dad was dealing with his own struggles and I felt like I couldn't talk to him. My little sister was three hours away in college. Ongoing drama with my external family left us on our own and I was detached from all of my friends after years of dealing with my own illness.

I couldn't understand why God was throwing all these obstacles my way. I couldn't get it. Why? We are good people.

The pain was again, too much to handle.

I internalized all the stress.

My mom and dad have always been there for me, and I wanted to be there for them too, but the energy, the negativity of the relationship, the negativity of the circumstances, the negativity of the environment in general was intense.

Stress is a direct cause of flare ups for my illness and shortly after this entire experience, after my mom and I moved out of the house I grew up in since I was in sixth grade, after we heard from my mom's doctor it was a false alarm (thank goodness), after our family dog suddenly passed away, after my dad got healthy again, I then got sick.

This was the sickest I've been yet with my autoimmune disease, and it lasted for eight long months. I had to quit my job working at a social media agency because I was too sick to be there every day. I couldn't leave my apartment for months at a time. To say it was an extremely difficult period of my life, is an understatement.

Day in and day out I'd cry, I'd feel the most intense pain. I'd not only be crying because of the physical pain or illness, but also because I was mourning the loss of the life I once had.

I couldn't understand why God was throwing all these obstacles my way

I don't blame anyone but myself for the recurrence of my illness. Even though I know blame is something we should never do as I mentioned earlier, I'm only human and at this time the internal blame got to me.

I knew stress caused flare ups.

I am the one who let the stress get inside of me. I am the one who allowed outside people, outside circumstances, and outside energy to affect me internally, even if I didn't realize what was happening at the moment.

This is when I realized I needed to protect myself

This is when I realized I needed to protect myself, because I saw the physical effects of letting external things get inside of me.

But how can you protect yourself when you can't run away from it?

Leave the people you love if they are causing you negativity. (You'll be surprised how many gurus or self-help teachers told me this.)

And I get where they are coming from; you must protect yourself at all costs and if you want to become this successful individual who truly lives a life of fulfillment and joy, you need to be very selective of who you choose to spend time with. But what do you do when those people are your entire heart?

What do you do if you have no place to go?

What do you do if you need support from others?

When you get into the details, most people can't just pick up and leave, especially if they have a family, or financial restraints, or responsibilities.

So, what do you do in these situations to protect yourself?

For me, I needed to be there for my mom and my dad, but I also needed to protect my own body so I wouldn't get sick again. (The last time I was sick, when nothing was working and I was on the last resort, my doctor said if I got really sick again, I would have to get surgery and live with a colostomy bag for the rest of my life.)

So, I created the invisible bubble.

I visualized myself surrounded by this big pink transparent bubble and when I was near people I loved who were going through their own struggles and hardship, I could sit there and be there for them. I could listen to them whether they were being understanding, negative, lashing out, or whatever it may be (as we all know we go through stages of grief when dealing with tragedy and hardship), and I can truly be there for them, but no longer would their energy affect me.

All that energy would come off of them and instead of getting inside of me, I visualized it bouncing off the bubble and disappearing into the ether.

I held this visualization at the front of my mind for years.

And I became, what I like to call, non-hackable.

No longer would outside events, circumstances, people, situations, environments, or whatever affect me.

I was now strong enough to be in the environment, not run away from it, and stay strong in my own healing energy.

The invisible bubble was my tool to protect my heart, my soul, and my body—all the while, still being close to the people who were my heart, and still are, my family.

I've tried running away from life before, it doesn't solve anything. It only causes more pain and heartache.

You can't run from your heart. You can't run from the things that you care about.

You have to face them, work through them, and hopefully come out of it a better individual. But it's not easy. Strength is necessary.

Resiliency isn't something you have, it's a muscle you build. All of your challenging experiences have built up that muscle for you to survive this far.

Try to remember every day, it is your job to protect your own supercomputer. You must work to become non-hackable.

Make it a priority.

Action Step: Visualize yourself in your invisible bubble, feel free to imagine any color that resonates with you. See how you feel. Notice how present you are yet how your energy is protected.

If it feels right to you, use this tool whenever you find the need. If the invisible bubble isn't resonating, make up your own tool. Maybe it's a box, a suit, or a shield you're holding. What if it's an imaginary sleeping bag you can step into and zip up to fully protect your energy? Whatever you can imagine yourself surrounded by, with ease, use that as your go-to tool.

Just like you protect your computer from malware or your passwords from hackers, let this tool act as a way to protect you during stressful or negative situations so you can become *non-hackable*.

CHAPTER TWENTY-THREE

The Fearful Leader

Feel the fear and do it anyway.

When you go through hard times, fear is there.

When you go through good times, fear is there.

When you live in this world, fear is there.

Too many people are controlled by unjustified fear; it is the puppet master to so many people's lives and they accept the role as the puppet. It tells you if you can or can't do something. It will make you think twice about going after something you love. It will cause you to live in paralysis, making you fear what may come through action. It allows you to live a lonelier life, too afraid to get vulnerable in front of others.

Fear is always there. It can control you or you can allow it to fuel you forward.

But the only way you can let it fuel you forward is by gaining real courage. Not waiting for the fear to pass, not waiting until you don't feel any fear, but feeling the fear and doing it anyway.

What you must understand is that,

Fear is inevitable but listening to that fear is a choice.

I've always been afraid.

I was afraid to raise my hand in class in middle school fearing what others may think or asking a question people would laugh at.

I was afraid to speak in public, in fear of messing up or forgetting all my lines.

Once I was diagnosed with ulcerative colitis, I was afraid of everything...

Afraid to go on long car drives, to get interviewed on live television, to be in the window seat on an airplane, to be on stage, to be out with friends, to be at someone else's house, to go on a date... all in fear I wouldn't make it to a bathroom on time.

I was living in a constant state of fear.

No matter how hard I tried, fear would be there, lingering over me.

There was this one time while living in South Florida getting ready to host the third Women Empower X conference that I got booked to be interviewed on the local CBS channel.

It was a morning interview and they requested I arrive at the TV station by 6:00 a.m., and I lived thirty minutes away.

I got up super early to make sure I had time for my bowels to start moving before I had to go on the road, as the mornings are always the worst. I didn't have time to wait at my apartment until I was confident I'd be okay. I was expected to be there on time.

I got in my car and drove myself there, the streets still dark.

During this thirty-minute drive, I tightly gripped the steering wheel with both hands and started saying, "Please God, let me make it there. Please God, let me make it there. Please God, please, *please*. I'm praying."

I didn't get a chance to think about the answers for my interview or the subject matter. I didn't get a chance to practice how I'd promote the event so people would see the TV spot and want to attend. I didn't have a chance to calm my mind and mentally prepare for a great first TV interview.

All I could do was feed into my fear.

> *"Oh, no, here it comes, the pain. I don't know if it's safe to stop somewhere in the dark on the highway. I don't have enough time to stop and still get there on time. Oh no, please God, please!"*

I continued to drive, hands clenched on the steering wheel, and my focus on praying.

I pulled up to the studio, praying someone would come outside quickly to let me in. Immediately when I saw someone I had to jump out of my car and ask them if I could first use the restroom before even introducing myself to them.

I ran to the bathroom almost in tears.

The interview went well, but of course I knew I could've done better if I just was able to calm myself and concentrate on the interview at hand versus listening to this fear.

But this was my new reality; fear would always win and fear was always there.

I've had this happen too many times to count.

Before one speaking gig in South Florida, I had to ask the organizer if I could switch time slots with someone in the afternoon because I didn't feel well and wouldn't be able to make it up on stage talking for an hour.

When I was speaking at a conference in NYC, I got a home rental with a few of the other speakers and there was only one bathroom in the place and five of us. I barely ate that entire weekend trip in fear I'd eat something that caused me to feel sick and someone else would be in the bathroom when I needed it.

I was so weak during that conference. I could barely eat at all because at that time, everything I ate other than some plain white rice upset my stomach. I couldn't digest any food.

I've had these experiences happen to me more than you probably can imagine. And through all of this, I was still building my brand as a public speaker and growing Women Empower X.

I was sick behind the scenes and sick in front of others, yet no one really knew. I talked about my autoimmune disease and shared my experiences, but when people see you on stage or on television or growing this big business, and you look "perfect" (since autoimmune diseases are invisible to the eye), they don't believe that you're still going through the tough times.

But I was, and it was extremely hard.

Every single day I was living in fear. Even today, fear strikes me at least once a day, whether it's regarding my autoimmune disease or fear I'm sure everyone can relate to: about our future, our dreams, our loved ones, money, and so forth. Fear is always present.

That's the thing, when you look at someone you admire, someone may be doing the thing you want to do, whether it's buying a van and traveling cross-country, quitting a 9-5 job to go all in on their dreams,

> *Every single day I was living in fear*

asking a crush out on a date, writing the book, speaking in public, or standing up for what a person believes in. The list could go on and on. Many believe those individuals doing the things—the thing YOU want to do—aren't afraid anymore, but that's simply not the truth.

We all have fears, just some people feed them more than others.

I don't believe there is such a thing as a fearless person or fearless leader.

If anything, I am a fear*ful* leader.

The way I've been able to achieve everything I have through all the fear I feel daily is through this mindset technique I taught myself.

I view the fear as a sign, a sign that if I'm afraid of it then obviously I care about it, and if I care about it, I know I will be that much more impactful doing it.

If I'm afraid of speaking in public, in fear of what others may think, I care about using my story to positively change people's lives.

If I'm afraid of staying in the same place in fear I will miss my chance to see the world, I care about seeing the world.

If I'm afraid of growing a business in fear of failing, I care about that dream.

When you feel fear, and no direct danger is present, ask yourself,

Is this fear fact or fiction?

More often than not, your fearful thoughts are fictional versus reality.

The fear I had that I wouldn't make it to the bathroom on time, fictional. I don't know if that will actually happen, it may or it may not. The fear was most definitely real, and something I'll be vulnerable to share I still deal with every time I go on a longer car drive, but more often than not, the fearful thought never comes true. If I want to continue to travel, pursue my dreams, and follow my passion I can't let this fear towards something that may or may not come true, stop me.

Fear you will mess up on your dream job interview, fictional. You may or you may very well not.

Fear you will fail if you decide to chase after your dreams. You may or you may very well not.

Feelings of fear, when it comes to internal unjustified feelings, are most of the time fictional; you don't know if it will actually happen, so don't ever let something that's not even real control your life!

People have always asked me how I started my business, how I became a public speaker and, in every question, people always include, "Weren't you afraid?"

I mean we were renting out some of the largest convention centers in the country as a new startup, of course I was afraid!

But I care about the work we set out to achieve. I care about who we are going to impact. I care about my own dreams and the dreams of others.

I was always afraid doing everything I've done my entire life but,

I fear regret more than I fear failure.

Action Step: Name one thing you are afraid to pursue and write that down in your journal. For example, this can be a dream job, starting your own business, or a relationship. Take some time to journal how *not* going after it would make you feel. If you didn't take any action to go after it, where would you end up? How would you feel? Will you be happy?

If there is any ounce of regret as you wrote out these feelings, use the saying "*I fear regret more than I fear failure*" and work up the courage to do it anyway. (And don't wait, this is your sign to get started TODAY!)

CHAPTER TWENTY-FOUR

Take Back Your Power

Have you ever experienced something that has *affected* you?

A challenge, an obstacle, a tragedy that has stuck with you, to the point where it *changed* you?

I asked a similar question one time while speaking on stage. I asked the audience to first close their eyes, and then I said, "Raise your hand if you're currently going through something that is *affecting* you." Emphasizing on the word, *affecting*.

The entire audience raised their hand. When people opened their eyes, tears began to stream.

When you are brave enough to be vulnerable and open up about your current challenges, you'll realize you're not alone. Everyone is walking around pretending like their life is "perfect" yet so many people are struggling behind the scenes.

And we're all too afraid to talk about it.

Now I don't mean to give the advice that you should always be talking about your problems, but what I do mean is to be open about them.

The more open you are, the less alone you will feel.

Vulnerability is a powerful thing because it gives you back your power.

When you hide your vulnerabilities, they have power over you. You hide them because you are too afraid to let others see them and that leads you to showing up inauthentically.

We aren't fully open and honest with ourselves or others because we are controlled by our vulnerabilities, always prioritizing them ahead of our own needs. To make sure, under all situations, they are hidden.

Think about when you go to meet new people, how many times do people ask, "What do you do?"

They never ask, "How are you?" "Who are you?" or "What's your passion?" These questions bring about more honesty; they bring about answers that will really get to know another person over just asking what's on their business card or resume.

That's one thing that's rooted in our company culture: we say WEX is a place where you share, not just what you do, but who you are.

Who you are is what will change the world and your vulnerabilities are part of that. They are what make you beautiful and unique.

When you hide them, you are hiding a part of yourself. When you aren't brave enough to show the world who you truly are, you'll never be able to fully live up to your potential.

◆◆◆

When I was struggling to try and heal both mentally and physically from my autoimmune disease and suffering from post-traumatic stress disorder, I went to different seminars where motivational speakers and authors would share their stories and advice.

I saw so many amazing and influential speakers and *NY Times* Best-Selling authors in the wellness and spirituality space. While all of them were very inspiring and knowledgeable, I always left these events feeling even worse about my current life.

When each person spoke, they all followed a similar pattern. They shared their story of challenging times they had experienced, from abusive parents to alcoholism to loss. Then they shared what they did to overcome these challenges and provided their solution and steps so we too can overcome any challenge.

For someone who is having a hard time getting over or through something that happened in their past, this advice would be transformational for them.

But for me, it just made me feel worse.

Living with a chronic illness, I'm never going to overcome this. There is no cure and it is not something that is just in my past. It's not something that *happened*, and now I can move forward.

My near-death experience is in my past. The post-traumatic stress I was suffering from as a result of that past experience is definitely something I can overcome, and I did. But the challenges I was facing with my new normal, living with a chronic illness is something I'm going to have to deal with for the rest of my life.

That's when I knew I had to share my story because I want people to know that you don't have to overcome something to do what you love in this world. You don't have to have it all figured out to inspire others. You don't have to have all your challenges in your past in order to be viewed as an influential leader.

When I speak on stage, I share my current struggles with my illness or the current struggles as a business owner. I share all my vulnerabilities because then, hopefully, if people see me on stage, sharing about something I'm currently going through, they too will see they have permission to do the same.

When we hide away our vulnerabilities, we won't ever truly be able to create those deep connections we are all longing for.

And, we will always be waiting, waiting until we overcome something in order to be someone.

You already are someone!

Let's face it, there will always be obstacles and challenges you are faced with. Some bigger than others. But regardless, life is never smooth sailing 100% of the time.

So why would you want to spend your entire life trying to overcome something? Who wants to do that?

Instead, turn that obstacle into an opportunity: an opportunity to get vulnerable in front of others, an opportunity to inspire others through your stories, an opportunity to create impact.

Find the opportunity through the obstacle. There is always one there.

Be vulnerable; accept who you are fully and give others the chance to accept the real you as well.

It is time to share your vulnerabilities. It is time to take back your power.

If I asked you to name all the things you love... how long would it take to name yourself?

Action Step: In your journal, write out one thing in your life, something that is very much part of who you are, that you've hidden from others.

Maybe it was your past childhood, mental health struggles, or imposter syndrome you're currently experiencing. After writing it out in your journal, find the courage to share your story with just one person who doesn't know this about you. It can be a close friend or family member to start, but get vulnerable and be open with them.

As the tears may shed, so will the weight you've been carrying all alone. You can hold on to this, trying to protect yourself from someone finding out but then you'll risk living a life fully boxed in, and always feeling alone. Or you can choose today to take back your power by sharing your vulnerabilities with others.

CHAPTER TWENTY-FIVE

Feeling the Feelings

I f you're an empathetic person, you'll be able to relate to this statement: Sometimes I feel sad and I don't know why.

Some people I've had conversations with around this topic can't understand. They think there is always a reason you are sad and you can figure out what that reason is. While to some extent they are correct, I don't think there is a need to *always* dig deep into your past or try and point out every little thing that's wrong in your life just to find out what that reason is.

I find myself asking "why" way too often when I'm not feeling myself or I'm feeling sad. I harp on that question like what I'm feeling is wrong or something.

◆ ◆ ◆

When I was going through years of struggle with my health, I knew why I wasn't happy each day. But then when I got healthy, and there were days I still felt a bit sad, I would be mad at myself for even feeling that way.

I'd say to myself, "You're healthy, your family is healthy, you waited for this for so long. Why are you sad? You have no right to be sad! You should be grateful."

And of course, that inner talk continued for as long as I'd allow it to and that just made me sink deeper into my low feelings.

This cause of sadness may be from deep-rooted trauma. Those memories sometimes don't present themselves as a thought but instead an internal feeling, spreading the hard feelings time to time throughout my mind and body.

Or maybe it's not my trauma at all that's causing this undetected sadness, but instead coming because I'm an empath. *Dang being an empath.*

Whatever the reason is, there are times when I feel worse about myself because I'm questioning *why* I feel this way when I *should* be happy.

Just because you don't feel happy though does not mean you are not grateful for your life and all you have.

Just because you don't feel happy does not mean you are depressed.

Just because you don't always *feel* happy does not mean you are not a happy person.

My high school physics teacher was a very intelligent man and to this day, I remember one powerful lesson he taught me. The first day of class he asked his students what the meaning of life is.

Students responded with answers of love, happiness, success, or other related terms.

He responded, "The meaning of life is joy."

Since I heard these words so many years ago, I've been trying to figure out this meaning.

What's the difference between happiness and joy?

What's the difference between happiness and joy?

After many years of heartache, struggle, and challenges, I finally understand.

> *After many years of heartache, struggle, and challenges, I finally understand*

Happiness is dependent on the moment. You can feel happy one minute and sad the next. But joy, joy is something internal. You can still feel joy in your life even when crying during a sad movie, feeling unhappy because you didn't achieve a goal, or just having an off day for no reason at all.

I can be sad and joyful. I can be happy and joyful. I can be a mix of all the hard feelings and not understand where they are coming from and still feel grateful for my health, family, and life.

I also understand though that timing matters when it comes to sad feelings.

What I mean by that is the longer you allow your sad feelings to sit with you, the more difficult it will become to rise above them towards happiness.

Feelings create patterns and memories inside our body.

If you feel sad for one day, it's easy to be happy the next day. But if you feel sad for one year, without having a direct reason to why you're feeling this way, it's going to be harder to just wake up one day and start feeling completely happy. (Note I said harder *NOT* impossible.)

That's why you must set a time limit for these harder feelings (And please note, I'm not talking about when a tragedy hits like a death or loss or anything that is a direct correlation to your feelings, I'm talking about those hard feelings that don't have a direct reason. These are the ones you continue to wonder why you are feeling them). When that time limit is up, you need to have tools in place to get you back on track towards more positive feelings.

For example, I have a go-to song that always puts me in a good mood, "The Tide is High" by Atomic Kitten. (Slightly embarrassing fact: It reminds me of my childhood days watching *The Lizzie McGuire Movie*.)

> *I'm sure you know, repressed feelings always have a way to come back and find you*

Through my journey I've also discovered a key trick to get to a feeling of happiness quicker and more often. That, to me, is the secret to living a happy life: **be happy more often than I am sad.**

It does not mean you need to be happy 365 days out of the year, but if you are happy more days than you are sad, you will always have a feeling of joy in your life, even on the sad days.

So, here's the trick: **When you feel sad, *stop* asking yourself why you feel sad. When you feel happy, *start* asking yourself why you feel happy.**

Flip the script.

I discovered this one day when I was laughing hysterically with my sister and it got to a point where we asked each other what we were even laughing about.

Then we started to work back through our conversation, which brought about more happiness because it was leading to this hysterical laughter!

Most of us question our feelings of sadness but never question our feelings of happiness. But what if we flipped it?

What if, when we are feeling "off" we just allow ourselves to feel that way. We feel the feelings but that's all.

We don't harp on *why* we are feeling them. And we most definitely don't push them away because as I'm sure you know, repressed feelings always have a way to come back and find you.

You feel the feelings and that is all.

Then when you're feeling happy or laughing, ask yourself why you are feeling that way.

You'll then spend more time thinking on the things, people, or experiences that are bringing you happiness and less time focused on all the sad things. Now you'll be more consciously aware of what you need to do to continue to bring happiness into your life.

Flip the script with yourself. It makes all the difference.

I've been feeling my feelings since 1991 and today, I'm grateful for every single one of them.

It may be a bad day, not a bad life.

Action Step: In your journal, follow the below steps:

1. Think about the last time you felt happy, now write down *why* you felt that way.
2. Create your happiness toolbox. List out some things that make you feel good. These are now your go-to tools for when your time is up on feeling those sad feelings.
   a. Some ideas for what to include:
      - A song or playlist
      - A book
      - A motivational YouTube video
      - Exercise or playing a sport
      - Meditation
      - Writing/Journaling

It's so important to spend some time creating your happiness toolbox as anytime you're feeling sad or down, you can then go to it and choose one thing to do in order to push through the hard feelings and bring about the good ones.

CHAPTER TWENTY-SIX

The "Shoulds" of Life

You should get a real job.

You should get married before you're thirty.

You should have kids when you're young.

You should spend more time with your family.

You should go to temple or church more.

You should, you should, you should, you should….

I'm so sick of all these "shoulds"!

How can life be filled with so many stipulations when life is always shifting and moving and everyone on this planet is different!

I don't get it… we are living this life of others' "shoulds" and making ourselves always feel bad for what we really want in life.

We think it's wrong if we don't want to get married right away. We are made to believe we are less worthy when we are single.

We are looked down upon if we don't have kids by a certain age or if we choose to pursue our dreams over finding a *stable* job with a 401k retirement plan.

I mean think how much we celebrate engagements, weddings, and baby showers. While they all call for a celebration, how come we don't equally celebrate when a woman starts her own business or lands a promotion?

I'd say that calls for just as big of a celebration from everyone, don't you?

All these *"shoulds"* only keep us from achieving what we are meant to achieve while here in this world.

We are held back by these societal standards. They do not keep us safe. They do not protect us from the tragedies that will come. They do not serve us in any way.

But we believe they will.

We are made to believe they will protect us from hardship so we follow them, yet what do we experience afterwards? More hardship.

The only way to truly experience the life you are meant to experience is by being aligned with your core purpose and no "should" set by someone else will ever be able to show you the way- the only "should" to listen to is the one told by your intuition.

I had been traveling for a straight eight hours and just landed in Sacramento, California for a speaking engagement. I was scheduled to speak to 800 sorority women at the University of California Davis Campus the next morning. After a long day of travel, all I like to do is check into my hotel, grab some food to go, and eat alone while watching reruns of *Friends* on TV in my hotel room.

I'm definitely not one of those people who sit at the bar alone or one to eat out alone. I've always admired folks who do that, I'm just not one of them.

After I checked into my hotel, took my suitcase up to my room, I headed back downstairs to the lobby where the restaurant was. (Travel tip: If the hotel has a restaurant that is run by them, you usually can order from the same menu as you would for room service as it comes from the same kitchen and they won't charge you that hefty room service fee. I'm a sucker for a good savings tip.)

Anyway, I went down to the restaurant and they had a bar where only one woman was sitting. She was dressed all in white; white pants, white shirt, and even a white scarf and had bleached blonde hair.

I didn't feel like talking to anyone so I ventured to sit a few seats away from her so I wouldn't have to get into small talk.

As I'm minding my own business looking at the menu, the woman in white asked me in her very strong southern accent, "Do you like cauliflower?"

I looked up to make sure she was talking to me as it was a very odd first question. No one else was around.

"Yes, but I can't eat it," I responded back.

"How come?" she asked.

Ugh, why are people so nosy I thought to myself.

"Dietary restrictions."

> *She was dressed all in white; white pants, white shirt, and even a white scarf…*

I probably was a bit shorter with her than I usually am but again, I had just been traveling for eight hours, my mindset wasn't in the best place after so many changes and challenges in a short amount of time, and I was exhausted.

The woman dressed in white continued to pry into my dietary restrictions mentioning she was curious because she did healing work. She also asked about the cauliflower because she wanted to order it but didn't think she'd eat the whole thing and was seeing if I'd be interested in sharing it with her.

I mentioned, "I have an autoimmune disease." I did not want to get into all the details nor talk about this with her but she continued to ask what autoimmune disease while apologizing for being invasive.

At least she was aware of what she was doing.

After I told her it was ulcerative colitis, I could tell she didn't know much about it, but then I was fully in a conversation with her and I just accepted the fact that there is no way of getting out of this situation until my food was ready and I could have an excuse to leave.

Ugh, I thought, *I should be resting right now or preparing for tomorrow's speaking gig. I should call my mom to tell her I got to the hotel safely. I should be checking my emails to see if anything urgent has come up for work.*

She led the conversation asking where I was from, quickly discovering we went to rival colleges, I went to the University of Florida and she, Florida State University.

She continued with the questions, now asking what I was doing in Sacramento and I explained how I'm a professional speaker and will be speaking at the university the following day on the topic of confidence. Since I was full in this conversation then, I finally posed a question her way and asked her what she does as a healer. She mentioned she focuses on women's empowerment, which of course led to my sharing of my company WEX and the work we do. I didn't go too in-depth, again I was not in a talkative mood, but just mentioned our company mission and purpose.

I didn't have a business card to give her when she asked for one, as all my stuff was upstairs in my hotel room, so I just wrote down my social media handle and website URL on my dinner receipt and handed it to her.

At this point I started to get a little weirded out as she would not stop staring into my eyes throughout the entire

At least she was aware of what she was doing

conversation. I mostly looked down or straight ahead during the silent moments as we were sitting at the bar and I wanted her to pick up my vibes of "I don't really feel like talking right now!" but she ignored those entirely. When I handed her my receipt, she just kept looking at me.

Alexa Carlin ··

She mentioned she was a medium and shared how she really focuses on helping guide her clients to do the work they are destined to be doing without getting into people's energy zones too much.

"I feel like you're really good at discernment and being able to tell who you can trust and who you need to stay away from to protect your energy," she said to me.

"I guess so?"

"I usually would be extremely tired and not want to talk to anyone as I wait for my food

> *You are not just good at what you do, you're the best at what you do*

here at the bar," she went on to mention, which took me by surprise as that's exactly how I felt. She continued, "but something felt different when you came up. That's why I continued to ask you questions."

I would like to say I was now feeling like this was a bit off but to be honest, I've had so many spiritual encounters with different people in unique situations that this didn't take me by surprise, and instead I welcomed what was to come next.

"I don't want to be too in 'your zone' but I want to share the messages I'm receiving. You are not just good at what you do, you're the best at what you do. I am so excited for you as you have a great future ahead. I see you at the top, as the 'mastermind' of it all. The work you are doing today is important, but it is on this level," showing her hand perpendicular to the floor at a low level.

"In the future you will be up here," raising her hand above her head.

"The master of it all and you will be leading people to new heights. Can I give you a hug? I don't want to be too in your zone, but I'd love to be able to give you a hug."

I nodded yes and we both stood up from sitting at the bar. No one else was in the restaurant other than the bartender who was back in the kitchen getting our food ready.

In the middle of this hotel lobby bar, we shared an oddly long hug and after what felt like three minutes, she put her hands on my shoulders, straightening out her arms to be able to now look at me and said, "You are so beautiful, you really are beautiful."

She took a deep breath and that was it.

Both of our to-go meals came out at this exact moment and I took my meal, said bye to her and rushed back up to my room to document this experience in my journal.

Now to be quite transparent with you, this is the third time I was out in public and a random, spiritual encounter took place where someone sought me out to tell me something. One time this happened in the parking lot at Whole Foods, another time it happened at a large tech event I was speaking at in Miami, Florida.

All three times the message, conversation, and experience were different but I now recognized the one thing they all had in common. They all were telling me messages I already intuitively knew.

I know I'm meant to do something bigger, yet society tells me I should be on this track. I should stay the path I'm on because I've already built momentum and I can one day maybe sell the company. I should focus on this idea because others are making a lot of money in this industry and I can too. I should be doing this now because once I have kids, I won't be able to.

> *"You are so beautiful, you really are beautiful"*

So many "shoulds" have prevented me from listening to my intuition. Sure, I've always listened and followed my passion but intuition and passion to me are very different.

Passion is what excites me, and it has been my passion that led me to speaking and founding Women Empower X, but intuition, well what my intuition tells me is much scarier. It is something less than one percent ever succeed at doing. It is something that is so far out there, people will laugh and say, well everyone wants that.

So, I've never gone after it. But here is this message yet again.

I've feared listening to my intuition but now writing this, I'm wondering why I am afraid to listen to myself, the person I should trust the most, yet I so easily listen to others?

Most people fear change because they don't want to get off the set path they've been told is the right path. They think if they go to school, graduate from college, get a good job, find someone to marry, start a family, and save for retirement that life will be perfect and simple.

Yet that is farthest from the truth.

You can choose to live by the "shoulds" of life set for you or you can choose to create your own path.

And when you choose to live by your own rules and standards, no longer will you be held back from fear of change.

We fear change because we think we won't know how to move through it; we want everything to stay the same so we don't have to find new ways of doing things.

Just because something was done a certain way in the past does not mean it's the best way to do it moving forward.

·· Adaptable

And that understanding is what will help you adapt and thrive through any change.

But in order to find that truth, in order to truly understand how to adapt and embrace the unknown is by letting go of all the things and ways you think you "should" be living your life.

There is not one set path to lead a good life. There is not one set answer to how to show up every single day and become the person you are meant to be.

Learn from others but ultimately, know you are in charge of your own life. The "shoulds" are there to make people feel safe and protected, but in the end, the same challenges will come.

The same change will come and you can keep the course you've always been on trying to solve new problems with old solutions, or you can change the world with your ideas and new ways.

Will you take the paddle and change course or will you keep floating by with the current of life?

Change happens for a reason, but the only way to discover that reason is to embrace it and learn to forge a new path. Learn to listen to yourself, what you intuitively know you *should* be doing.

Growth only comes from change and to adapt to that change and rise above, you must rid others' "shoulds" of life and use your own intuition to guide the way to develop new solutions.

Be open to it. Embrace it. And never ever be held down by the "shoulds" others are creating for you.

So, will you decide to change the world?

Action Step: Write down all the "shoulds" others have set for you. Whether those have been set by society, by the media, or by your parents and friends. After you make a full list, writing every single one down, look at it. Then cross every single sentence off. Remove them from your vocabulary. Stop living by someone else's rules; create your own.

Now, take a moment and dig deep down. Is there something your intuition has been trying to tell you, yet you've been ignoring it or maybe too afraid to listen to it? Know that message, that feeling, that is the very thing you need to listen to, the only thing you *should* be doing that will lead you to where you are meant to be.

Write that thing down in your journal and commit yourself to chasing after it.

CHAPTER TWENTY-SEVEN

Set Your Non-Negotiables

Pivoting does not equate to failure. Pivoting is simply a shift in direction to get to your desired destination.

Sometimes we will choose to pivot based upon our own desire to change the journey we are on, but most of the time, we must pivot as a result of some circumstance.

While that should be a positive thing, the ability to adapt to change and choose a new path in order to get to a desired result, pivoting today has become so closely connected and intertwined to feelings of failure or feelings of not being good enough. This to me is a result of viewing the reason to pivot in the wrong way.

We pivot because we feel we have to.

We pivot because we "failed" at the current path we were on.

We pivot because society is telling us to.

When we look at our need to pivot from these perspectives, we may head too far off course or we may lose faith in ourselves.

We must face that sometimes life doesn't go as planned, and in order to continue to rise to the occasion and achieve what we want in life we must be able to adapt to things thrown our way, which includes pivoting along our journey.

But with that pivot, we must never take the victim seat and work in survival mode, but instead choose to always be the leader of our own life.

When you pivot in a mindset of survival mode, what ends up happening all too often is you start to feel resentment towards your dreams. You're doing everything you can to make it work, but it just isn't working, and now you feel the only option is to pivot towards a path you really don't want to be on.

Now the concept here is not whether you should pivot. As mentioned previously, we must always be able to adapt to changes thrown our way which includes pivoting to survive, but the key difference here is ensuring your mind is in the right place before you choose which way to pivot.

Instead of basing your decision on surviving, make a decision based on your *purpose*.

When you pivot based on outside factors (i.e., what others are telling you to do, in response to a negative circumstance, or what society deems as giving you better odds at being successful), you'll likely run into one or more of the following:

1. You'll discover you're not having fun anymore while growing what used to be your dream.
2. You'll become burnt out a lot quicker.
3. You'll begin to feel resentment towards your dream.

Instead of following what others are telling you is a logical solution and responding to the negative feelings coming up that result from having to even pivot in the first place, follow what you *know* deep down is right for *you;* based on your heart, your passion, and your intuition.

This is when logic and intuition go head-to-head, and it is your job to listen to the latter.

I mean just look at what happened in 2020 when the pandemic hit… hundreds of thousands of business owners, including myself, were forced to pivot in a new direction.

We all quickly acted in survival mode and ended up putting a band-aid on the situation, thinking this negative circumstance will only last a short time.

But that band-aid slowly started to come off as the pandemic lasted longer and longer.

Business owners became burnt out, they lost their passion, the band-aid wasn't a sustainable business strategy after a while, and many businesses unfortunately had to close their doors.

But there were a few businesses that pivoted during this time towards something that was still aligned with their core mission, still aligned with their purpose, and those businesses rose to the top and not only survived the pandemic, but thrived through it.

For example, two artists, a sculptor and a curator from Mexico City were out of work when the pandemic hit, so they started baking and using food to continue to create art and share it with the world on social media. What turned out to be a quarantine hobby led them to a thriving bakery business.

> *We all quickly acted in survival mode and ended up putting a band-aid on the situation*

While baked goods and creating sculptures and curating art is very different, they succeeded because their purpose was aligned. Whether it was food or using other materials, the two artists were creating things that people enjoyed, that put a smile on other's faces. That was their core purpose as an artist all along.

So how do you find the solution of where to pivot when you are so focused on the path you are on today without getting into the negative mindset of doubt, fear, or uncertainty?

The answer: You set your non-negotiables.

◆◆◆

When I was in the dating world, I spent so much time going out on dates with the wrong guys. If I enjoyed my time with the guy, I'd always think, *Well, I should give them a second chance and go on another date.*

Date after date I felt like I was wasting my time

The problem with that is, I can pretty much get along with anyone and have a good time with anyone because I enjoy my own company. (And laughing during a date is always a sign that you're having a good time except I later realized, I make myself laugh.)

During this stage though, I wasn't looking for another casual date or just a boyfriend, I was looking for "my person." I was ready for a commitment and the time I did have available outside my business I wanted to spend with my family and friends, not dating someone that was just a fling.

Date after date I felt like I was wasting my time and spending so much energy on guys that deep down I knew weren't the one.

Until I set my non-negotiable list.

What is a non-negotiable list, you may ask? It's exactly what it sounds like, it's all the things someone *must* possess in order for them to be the right person for you.

This list was like my bible when it came to dating. If a guy I went on a date with didn't have something that was on this list, I knew right away they couldn't be "my person."

Here was my Non-Negotiable Dating List:

1. They have to support my dreams.
2. They have to be sweet, kind, and compassionate. (This was a big one for me because I always had the fear of sharing my autoimmune struggles with someone.)
3. They have to be smart and make me laugh.
4. They have to be driven and motivated.
5. They need to be family-oriented.
6. They want to travel and see the world.

The list continued to about ten items.

Every time I went on a date after writing this list, I would reference it, now having a better idea if this person I'm meeting will be someone I should continue spending time with and getting to know or not.

It helped differentiate the things that would be a "nice-to-have" vs. a "must-have."

For example, it would be great if the guy was into finance and tech, was worldly, and had a sister close to my age I could be friends with. But these were not non-negotiables, rather just items on a list that would be great, but not necessarily the key factors to finding the person I wanted to spend the rest of my life with.

Another example which is something I discovered while writing this list was that I didn't *need* the person to be well-traveled, but before this exercise I always thought I needed that. I looked for someone who had cool experiences to share from their travels like I did but after really sitting down and thinking about my core needs, it wasn't that I needed a well-traveled man, I just needed someone who would *want* to travel and see the world. There's a big difference there!

> *Every time I went on a date after writing this list, I would reference it*

This non-negotiable list ended up leading me to my husband shortly after writing it, so it proved to be very effective.

Why am I sharing this with you?

When the pandemic hit, as I mentioned, I was forced to pivot in my business just like so many others in order to survive. Before the pandemic, my entire business was an in-person events company where we'd host conferences in convention centers around the country attracting 2,000+ women (obviously not an option anymore).

So, when this happened, and I had to cancel or postpone my events as well as my speaking engagements as a result of something out of my control, I had to figure out a way to bring in money.

This is where I was pivoting in *survival mode*.

There were a lot of ideas that came to mind to hold us over based on what others were sharing and based on external factors. Some ideas that I began to pursue while in this survival mode:

- An e-commerce drop-shipping store
- Creating content & finding influencer gigs on TikTok
- 1:1 coaching
- Affiliate marketing

I started to pursue each of these ideas until I began feeling resentment towards my dreams. I felt like everything I'd worked

> ### *It was like COVID-19 stole my dreams*

so hard for had been taken from me, and as a result, I was working on things I was not completely aligned with.

It was like COVID-19 stole my dreams.

This wasn't the first time I felt this way. When I was moving home from New York City back in 2014 due to my illness, I wrote in my journal that *my autoimmune disease stole my dreams.*

But COVID-19 did not steal my dreams nor did my autoimmune disease.

These circumstances (yes, they were the *reasons* I had to pivot in the first place), led me to discovering a better path, the journey I'm supposed to be on to achieve my purpose. But the only way I was able to perceive these negative circumstances that way was to understand the choices I had when it came to pivoting.

Remember, you can pivot in survival mode or you can pivot with purpose.

The cause may be the same (something out of your control) or maybe the cause is something within your control like having to pivot because your business isn't producing enough cash flow; either way, whatever the cause, you choose how you want to respond. That's what makes the difference.

Negative thoughts bring out a negative response which leads you to making decisions that are out of alignment with your intuition.

When my illness and the start of the pandemic came into my life, I viewed both of these circumstances negatively and blamed them for my dreams not being able to come to fruition. Through that belief, I was a victim to circumstance. I chose to pursue other things thinking that was the only way I could survive. I quickly felt the passion fade from my business and dreams. I felt defeated. I felt burnt out.

I chose to pursue other things thinking that was the only way I could survive

After a few months pursuing all these different things during the pandemic that were not aligned with the core mission of WEX, and feeling so much negativity around my business, I stopped myself and thought about another way.

This is when I began to write a list of what was really important to me when it came to my dreams.

As I began to write, I remembered the non-negotiable list I wrote for dating.

I thought, why don't we set non-negotiables when it comes to our business and dreams? Aren't they as important as finding the person we will spend the rest of our lives with? I mean, isn't this the career I want to spend the majority of my time working on for the rest of my life?

So, I started to write…

"My Non-Negotiables in My Business List":

1. Focused on empowering people to pursue their dreams.
2. Rooted in collaboration over competition.

3. Must always over-deliver in value.
4. Focused on diversity and inclusion.
5. Must allow freedom for me in my personal life.
6. I have to feel excited about it.
7. It needs to allow me to continue speaking and sharing my story.
8. Must be sustainable for long-term growth.

So, there it was: my non-negotiables when it came to my dreams.

I sat there, looking at this list in my home office and realized, there was nowhere on this list that I wrote, "in-person events" or even "in-person speaking engagements."

Those weren't non-negotiables for me. That was the path I was on yes, but looking at this list I realized there are so many other paths that I can pivot towards that would include all of these things that are important to me.

There are so many ways to empower people to pursue their dreams or to share my story.

Be open to change and be committed to your purpose. When you focus on your purpose, and less on the path, you'll most likely pivot towards the direction of your dreams.

This list helped me really get clear on what was important to me, what I wanted to create in this world, and brought me back to my core "why."

From there, it was easy to decide on a new path to pivot towards that I felt passionate and driven to make it happen. This led me to pursuing everything my team and I are doing today to positively impact people all over the world.

No longer was I pivoting in survival mode but instead, I was changing the road to get to the same destination.

Think of it like this; you are driving in a car and you decide to take one road all the way there to get to your destination. You are set on this path but suddenly there's a crash up ahead causing you to find a different route. You are frustrated, mad, and scared all at the same time because you don't want to go another way, you want to continue on this road.

But you can't and it's out of your control so you must choose to find a different road.

At this moment you see cars all merging off to one road that the officer handling the crash is leading people towards. But there are a few other roads nearby you can choose to take.

Now you are faced with a choice: follow others along the road because people are telling you it's the next best route or you can choose to get out of survival mode and take a moment to think on the real reason you were on that path in the first place.

Were you on that road because you wanted to see the mountains while driving or to stop in little towns to explore on your way there or was it to get to a certain destination the quickest?

When you can tap into your end goal in mind, that's when you'll be able to make the right decision for you and with that decision, you'll own it and not feel negative around this change in course.

The road may be different yes, but the driver is still you and the car can still be your core purpose. As long as you stay true to yourself and your purpose, you'll end up finding the next right path to take that will not only lead you to your core destination, but will have you enjoying the journey along the way.

> *You'll also feel more empowered when it comes to making decisions around your dreams*

Set your non-negotiables for your life and career before you begin to pivot. Get clear on what is important to you in your life.

When you are clear about what you want, the road seems to find you.

You'll also feel more empowered when it comes to making decisions around your dreams.

There's this phrase called the "shiny-object syndrome" which basically means you get caught up with trying to pursue the tactic, path, idea, etc. other people are dangling in front of you.

For example:

I just made $100k this month through Shopify, anyone can do it and I'll show you how.

These young entrepreneurs are bringing in millions through drop shipping and it's so easy you can too.

With just a few videos, you can make millions in your sleep through online courses.

Examples like these are endless.

There will always be these "shiny objects" put in front of you and if you give in to them, and redirect your focus off your core purpose, you'll find yourself weeks or months later on the wrong path and re-trying to figure it all out again.

Stay focused on your goals and your desires.

Know what's important to YOU in your life because that's what will ultimately direct you on the right path.

And if you can't seem to decipher between if it's a "shiny-object" you're chasing or actually part of your purpose, and whether you should be pivoting towards it now or not, ask yourself these questions:

1. Is this aligned with something on my non-negotiable list?
2. Do I have the resources right now to make it a success?
3. Is this urgent to do right now or can it be done later?

If the answer is yes to all three, go after it. If the answer is no or that it's not urgent right now, write it down in an idea journal to save it for later. The key is to stay focused on one thing at a time while building towards the grander vision you have for your life, based on the non-negotiables you set for yourself.

Don't follow others. Don't respond to circumstance by straying away from your vision. Try to view the situation in a positive light.

I mean looking back on my journey, if it wasn't for my autoimmune disease, the very circumstance I thought stole my dreams away from me and caused me to pivot, I wouldn't have ever gone on to inspire thousands of people through my stories and speeches or I wouldn't have ever founded Women Empower X.

> *Know what's important to YOU in your life*

I truly believe things happen for a reason, but I also know it's very difficult to see what that reason is while you're in the middle of the struggle. That's why it's so important to perceive the situation differently, so you don't end up giving up. The pivot can lead you to where you are meant to be.

There's not a need to struggle or fill your mind with negativity from the obstacles you experience along your journey. You may not always be able to control the path nor the challenges but you can always decide how you choose to react to those challenges.

Choose to be the leader of your own life and always choose to pivot with purpose.

Nothing and no one can steal your dreams away from you, other than you. The only way your dreams are stolen is by your deciding to give up on them, by deciding to give up on yourself. And one must never do that because the world needs what only you have to offer.

Action Step: In your journal, describe a time where you had to pivot out of survival mode. What did you do, where did that first lead you, how did you feel along the journey?

After reflecting upon this experience, work to create your non-negotiable list for your dreams. This can be your dream life or dream career, or a mix of both! Write out the list detailing the things that are most important to you. Remember these items must be mandatory for you, not just a "nice-to-have."

After looking at the list you just wrote, think back to the time you reflected upon where circumstances led you to pivoting. How could you have pivoted with purpose during this time instead of being in survival mode if you based it on your non-negotiables?

Now write out some ideas of new paths you can take that are aligned with your core purpose for what you want in your life.

Choose one to start. Use the three questions below to help you make a confident decision of which path to pursue:

1. Is this path aligned with my non-negotiables?
2. Do I have the resources right now to make it a success?
3. Is this urgent or can I pursue it later on my journey?

The one path that aligns with all three above is the one you should focus on.

CHAPTER TWENTY-EIGHT

Expectations

E very time you set an expectation, you are setting yourself up for disappointment.

Expecting things from others or expecting a certain outcome only leads to anxiety, frustration, anger, depression, and negative feelings.

We experience more peace, more happiness, when we let go of expectations.

Many times, when you feel frustrated in a relationship with someone, it's due to expectations you had that they didn't meet.

When you feel disappointed around an experience, it's due to an expectation again not being met.

Life is way too short to be setting all these expectations to only feel let down and less appreciative of what is actually happening in the moment.

Everything is based on your perspective, and you can literally change your entire life (aka your perspective) by shifting your expectations.

Think about it: if someone grew up wealthy and in an affluent family always visiting 5-star hotels and flying first class, but they one day stay at a 3-star hotel, and don't receive the same service they expect, they are going to perceive this experience as a disappointment. They may even write a bad review about the hotel because they didn't have or do xyz.

Now let's take this same example except this time, the person who is visiting the 3-star hotel grew up in a household that was living paycheck to paycheck and they've never experienced a 3-star hotel so they have zero expectations. They would most likely perceive every experience there as amazing and feel so appreciative for even the small things like having their room clean every night they are staying there.

Same experience. Two different people who have two different expectations. One is leading to disappointment; the other is experiencing the present moment of happiness and gratitude.

It's time to do away with expectations.

Now of course that's easier said than done.

I find myself setting expectations for everything. For example, I find myself setting a certain expectation of people's reactions to my stories.

When I share an exciting moment that happened at work with a friend or whomever, and the person who I'm sharing it with doesn't react with a certain sense of joy or excitement I was expecting back, bam- there comes the frustration.

I realized expectations were controlling my happiness when I had the biggest disappointment of all time; the disappointment of outside factors not fulfilling me as I had expected.

I dreamt for years what it would be like to get paid to travel as a speaker. I always said, "Just wait until I get there in my career, then I'll be super happy."

I *expected* the glamour of traveling, of speaking in front of large audiences all over the country, to fulfill me in some way but after a year of being on the road as a professional speaker, I realized I was getting more depressed.

Not because anything was wrong. I was inspiring thousands of people, making good money, and doing what I loved, but I was sinking into a state of depression because I wasn't feeling the fulfillment I *expected*.

Same thing for when I finally got healthy. I used to say, "Wait until I get healthy again and get into remission with my autoimmune disease, then I'll be happy every day."

Nope.

That didn't meet my expectations either. Because as we all know, obstacles follow obstacles.

Nothing fulfilled me the way I hoped it would and that, to me, has been the biggest disappointment of all time, especially when it came from my career or love life.

I had to learn the hard way that the only way to feel truly fulfilled is through inner work. Nothing and no one will ever fill that void for you except you and your faith.

Stop measuring your life by external factors and start measuring it on the internal plane.

The more you set expectations of others or experiences, the more you are setting yourself up for disappointment.

The key here is to catch the expectation as you are making it and choose to get rid of it.

Choose to be open minded and not attach any strings to anything.

Now that does not mean you don't want the best for you. Setting standards and expectations are two very different things.

Here's an example of the difference between expectations and standards. Imagine you are going on a first date with someone.

Setting high expectations: You imagine them having the entire night planned ahead of time with reservations at one of the best restaurants in town. They arrive dressed super nice and pick you up with flowers in hand. When you get to the restaurant, they order you a drink, remembering your favorite from conversations you had via text before the date… and so on.

Setting your standards: You are looking for someone who is kind to you, kind to the waiter, and kind to others. One who will take interest in you when you talk, really listening to what you have to say. Someone who is family-oriented, determined, and makes you laugh.

Two very different bars set. One will only let you down. The other will lead you to finding your person, regardless of what restaurant you visit.

Set your standards. Lose your expectations.

◆◆◆

As I'm writing this it's the Fall of 2020 and we are living through a horrible pandemic. This pandemic really showed us how much we rely on outside factors to fulfill us. We set expectations for 2020—big ones—and every single one of them brought upon a sense of disappointment.

College graduations were cancelled. Weddings didn't happen. Going out for a drink with friends—a thing of the past; everything we imagined for our year was stolen away by an invisible disease.

It's normal to feel sad from this experience. It's normal to feel disappointed that you didn't get to do everything you imagined this last year (or even longer now), and it's normal to let these outside circumstances affect your state of mind.

But what if we didn't have any expectations for the year; how much would we be able to adapt to the changes brought upon us?

That's how I want you to view every year ahead. Welcome change. Be grateful every single day you are still breathing.

It is truly the greatest gift of all time.

I got my breath taken away from me when I was in a coma, and I promised myself I would never live a day without feeling grateful for every breath I take.

This simple act of gratitude has the potential to help you return to the present moment and to what's most important.

You.

And your life here while you have it.

Whether you are living at home in a pandemic or traveling the world, when you lose the expectations, you can experience both as equally beautiful.

It's an experience in your life; you get to live it and you get to ultimately choose how it will affect your feelings.

We tend to feed our obstacles and starve our opportunities.

I'm asking you to flip it. Feed your opportunities and starve your obstacles.

Pay more attention to everything you CAN control.

Choose to lose your expectations so you can truly enjoy the moments that come your way.

Be grateful for everything in your life.

There is so much possibility for you. There is so much joy to be found.

You are here for a reason and that reason deserves to be recognized by you.

Wherever you are in the world reading this, know you are not alone.

Action Step: Think about the last time you felt disappointed because of someone or something not meeting an expectation. Write out this experience in your journal to discover the feelings that come up as a result of an expectation not being met and what kind of experience that led you to having.

When you can recognize the feelings that come up from expectations not being met, that's when we can begin to replace those feelings with a sense of gratitude.

After reflecting upon that moment, now write a list of all the expectations you have set for your personal and professional life (be honest with yourself, no one is going to see this but you!). Once you write all your expectations down on paper, read through that list and remind yourself to release those expectations the next time they come up.

When you find yourself setting an expectation, stop it in the thought process. Instead, replace it with, *"I will have zero expectations around this, and I will let life unfold how it's meant to, being happy right now, in the present."*

The next time you catch yourself in the moment and replace an expectation with the above thought, notice how the experience changes. Come back to this page in your journal and describe how the situation unfolded and your feelings around it. Now notice the difference of this experience from the one you previously described.

CONCLUSION

This is Just the Beginning

Your life can change at any moment. For the better or for the worse. That is not something you should be afraid of. It is something that makes life so wonderful, exciting, and exhilarating. You can't possibly know what the future holds for you. All you can do is keep going.

Keep going.

Never give up.

Never give up on yourself, on your dreams, and on the ones you love.

Just keep on keepin' on.

It isn't always easy, that's what your community is there for.

You won't always know what the next right step to take is, that's what mentors are there for.

There will be hard days, that's what your happiness tool kit is there for.

You may lose hope, that's what your curiosity is there for.

Your fears may stop you from taking action on your dreams, that's what I'm there for.

Change your perception and perspective of the world and your life will change. You have what it takes to keep going. Never doubt that. Never doubt your ability, your worth, your strength, or your intuition.

If I said to you, you have a one-percent chance of achieving your dreams, would you go after them? Majority would confidently say, *No way! Why would I risk my life on something where the odds are stacked against me?*

This is where you really have to have faith in yourself because let me ask you, why can't you be that one-percent?

The doctors gave me a one-percent chance to live. If my doctors, my family or my friends just said, *Well the odds are against her so there's no way she would survive,* I wouldn't be here today.

Believe you are the one-percent!

Put yourself in that category.

There is power in the underdog. There is power in defying the odds.

I've made it my life's mission to help people see that they deserve to be in the one-percent. I'm here to help guide you, cheer you on, and support you as you pursue your dreams.

I'd love to continue this journey with you as I truly believe that for you,

this is just the beginning.

Stay connected with me at @AlexaRoseCarlin across social media and learn more at AlexaCarlin.com.

Now go out into the world and lead with curiosity, pivot with purpose, and thrive through any change. I believe in you and I'm rooting for you.

Acknowledgments

This book wouldn't have been possible without the love, support, and encouragement of so many. First and foremost, I want to thank my community, the WEX Nation. Your continuous support and belief in me literally saved my life through some of my darkest days. Because you showed up for me, you gave me the strength to continue to show up for you. I am forever grateful for you and know this book wouldn't have been possible without your belief in me and my dreams.

Thank you to my wonderful partner in life, Colby. I'm forever grateful my feet led me to you. You are a real-life example that our darkest moments are what bring miracles in our future. Thank you for supporting me through all my emotional ups and downs while writing this book. And thank you for always helping me find faith and trust along the way, for believing in me even at times when I doubt myself, and for doing everything you can to help me make my dreams come true.

Thank you to my mom, for being by my side through it all: for giving me the gift of confidence, for giving me strength when I didn't have any, for being my caretaker through all my years of illness, and for always supporting my dreams and helping me believe in myself. Thank you for being strong for our family and for being my best friend.

Thank you to my dad, for helping me start my first business when I was just 17 years old and for being a pure example of what it means to persevere and never give up on your dreams. Thank you for always supporting me, guiding me, and teaching me how to stay optimistic even through some of the hardest times.

Thank you to my beautiful little sister, Julia, for showing me how to be strong and resilient. Thank you for never giving up on me and never giving up on yourself. I'm forever grateful to have you as a lifelong best friend.

Thank you to Angela Ribbler, who was by my side through many stories shared in this book. I don't know what I'd do without you. Thank you for all the adventures, the memories, and the unconditional love. And to the rest of the Wolfpack, Lauren Olesky and Jordan Solomon, thank you for showing me what true friendship looks like. I don't know what I would have done without you three while in college, during my near-death experience, and today, as we embark on this new chapter in our lives. Thank you for always making me laugh and bringing so much light and positivity into my life.

The creation of this book was only made possible by my incredible publishing team. Thank you, Michelle Vandepas for approaching me to write a book and giving me this incredible opportunity. Thank you to Karen Curry Parker for working with me through my endless ideas and coaching me through the entire writing process. Thank you to my talented editor, Laurie Miller Knight for your patience and commitment to helping me make this book the best it can be. And to the entire GracePoint family for all your hard work and dedication to make this book a reality.

A special thanks to Debra Gloria, for always helping me see my full potential and for showing me the power of sharing my authentic, vulnerable self. And of course, thank you for taking the photo for the front of this book cover! I'd also like to thank Andrea Bochner for believing in me and for your commitment and support to growing Women Empower X.

Thank you to each and every person who has been part of my journey thus far. To all my mentors, spiritual leaders, and friends who have impacted my life along the way, I am forever grateful for each one of you.

About the Author

Alexa Carlin is an in-demand public speaker, TV personality, and founder & CEO of Women Empower X (WEX), the premier community for women entrepreneurs. Alexa uses her infectious energy and courageous spirit to empower women to turn their obstacles into opportunities and pursue their dreams. Genuine by nature, caring at heart, and always inspirational, Alexa's vulnerability allows her to authentically connect with diverse women around the world, helping them understand the true potential they hold. Her company, Women Empower X, helps women entrepreneurs grow their businesses and brands through WEX's cutting edge courses, events, and publishing division, WEX Press. Alexa Carlin has worked with Fortune Global 500 brands to create captivating and relatable content and has been featured on the Oprah Winfrey Network, Cheddar TV, FOX, ABC, CBS, TEDx and in *Entrepreneur, Glamour* magazine, and *Forbes* among others. From a one percent chance to live to now being on a mission to make a difference in one person's life a day, Alexa is creating ripple effects of change for women everywhere. Residing in Raleigh, NC, Alexa shares her journey on AlexaCarlin.com and loves to connect to her followers @AlexaRoseCarlin on social media.

If you loved this book, you'll love this free gift even more!

Scan the QR code below or visit AlexaCarlin.com/adaptable to receive a free gift to help you on your journey towards becoming *Adaptable*!

You'll also be able to get a behind the scenes look into many of the stories shared within the book.

Stay connected with me at @AlexaRoseCarlin across social media and learn more at AlexaCarlin.com.

Now go out into the world and lead with curiosity, pivot with purpose, and thrive through any change. I believe in you and I'm rooting for you.

WEX Press is the official imprint of Women Empower X. We're committed to publishing women of diversity whose experiences and perspectives enlighten and inform others in business, inspiring them along the way.

WEX Press provides an opportunity for successful and up-and-coming women in business to share their expertise. WEX Press's exclusive book imprint produces top-quality non-fiction books with the same purpose and vision you've come to know and love through Women Empower X initiatives.

WEX Press offers the distribution and brand recognition of a traditional press while still allowing authors full rights to their own work. The line features titles from business professionals, entrepreneurs, speakers, and coaches with inspiring stories.

Do you have a book you've been dying to write,
a story you want to share, or lessons you
know will change others' lives?
If so, submit your book idea at
WomenEmpowerX.com/wexpress for consideration.

WEX PRESS
womenempowerX.

For more great books, find Wex Press online at
https://gracepointpublishing.com/wex-press/

Made in the USA
Middletown, DE
10 February 2022

60961655R00156